DECENTRALISED GOVERNANCE AND PANCHAYATI RAJ

DECENTRALISED GOVERNANCE AND PANCHAYATI RAJ

K.K. Srivastava

KALPAZ

Decentralised Governance and Panchayati Raj

ISBN: 978-81-7835-910-6

Published in 2011 in India by
Kalpaz Publications
C-30, Satyawati Nagar,
Delhi-110052
E-mail: kalpaz@hotmail.com
Phone : 9212729499

Lasser Type Setting : Quick Media, Delhi
Printed at : Chawla Offset Printers, Delhi

Dedicated to my Amma

Contents

Preface

For the success of democracy, decentralized governance is a must and for that the Panchayati Raj Institutions (PRIs) are the best example. Despite various attempts made by the government to bring about improvement in the health of PRIs (setting up of Working Group on District Planning, 1984, Committee on Administrative Arrangements for Rural Development, 1985, the L.M. Singhvi Committee of the Department of Rural Development, Government of India, 1986 and the introduction of 64th Constitutional Amendment in 1989). The position by and large remained unchanged till the passage of the 73rd Constitutional Amendment Act, 1993.

The 73rd Amendment has been hailed as a major landmark in the history of Local Self–Government in India. Some of the salient features of the Amendment are : grant of constitutional status to PRIs, reservation of one third of seats for women in panchayat bodies, holding of elections to panchayats after every five years under the direct supervision of the Chief Electoral Officer, setting up of Finance Commission to review the financial position of panchayats.

In the context of reservation policy for women in Panchayati Raj Institutions, it becomes pertinent to analyze their socio–economic status along with political accountability which was entrusted by constitution to them. The present book is based on the study on decentralized governance and problems of elected women representatives in Panchayati Raj to explore the findings and make remedial measures, lest it should not be known as will–o–wisp in the name of landmark constitutional amendment.

Acknowledgements

During the course of study, a considerable number of people have helped me owing to which I have been able to complete this work. I, therefore, gratefully acknowledge the contribution of each and every person. First of all, I am personally indebted to Prof. Emeritus Dr. S.N. Singh, Director, Institute for Applied Research and Development and reverend teacher for his dynamic advice, guidance and most valuable elderly concern for accomplishing this project. I very personally and humbly feel obliged to Prof. K. Kishore, Department of Public Administration, University of Lucknow for valuable advice and discussion from her administrative and academic busy time schedule. I also acknowledge the contribution made by Prof. I.D. Mishra in terms of his valuable guidance and suggestions. I am also thankful to Indian Council of Social Science Research (ICSSR), New Delhi for providing financial assistance for the study. I am also thankful to the officials of states, districts and blocks who directly and indirectly helped during the course of study.

My special thanks are to the members of the research team especially Dr. S.S. Chauhan, who took immense pain from his too busy schedule to complete the field work in time and later in compilation and tabulation of the data.

I would like to thank the library staff of the Department of Public Administration, University of Lucknow, particularly Sri. Y.P. Singh, Sri. Swarup Kishore and Sri. Mayank Srivastava for their sincere cooperation and encouragement in completing the work at the earliest.

Thanks are also due to Dr. A.K. Singh for conceiving the project and providing all types of support to complete the work. I am also thankful to Dr. Nimish Gupta for providing all types of technical support in processing data and compilation of book.

Last, but not least, I express my gratitude to all those who helped me particularly my collegues and friends.

1
Panchayati Raj Institutions in India: An Overview

Panchayati Raj in Ancient India

The village has always remained the most important unit of our social and economic life. It has naturally constituted the primary territorial unit of administration ever since very ancient times. Local government is deeply rooted in Indian history. The excavations in Mohanjodaro and Harappa of Indus valley civilization (3000 B.C.) speak volumes of the organized life in ancient times and reveal that they were amongst the oldest planned governing and planned system. Villages are very frequently referred to in the Vedas. The Jataka stories depict a faithful picture of the village life in India. From these stories, one can easily portray the rural administration and management. The importance of villages in Indian administration is attributable to the fact that the vast majority of Indian population 74 percent according to 2010 census lives in villages even now. It is well established fact that since very ancient times to the beginning of the 21st Century, not less than seventy percent of the population of India lived in villages. In the early Vedic times, the villagers themselves managed the simple affairs of the village, but the states being small, there was hardly any distinction between the central and local government. Villages were completely self governing. They were practically free from central control. The Gramini (headman) and other village officials were appointed by the community and were accountable to them.

Since ancient times the village has been the pivot of administration and the real centre of social life around which the entire structure of local self government revolved with facility and ease. Groups of villages were formed for undertaking those works of public utility and welfare which could not be economically or efficiently undertaken by a single village; example inter–village bridges, roads and other means of transport. The manifold functions of these ancient institutions comprised not only the normal civic duties but embraced all conceivable kinds of public affairs, industrial and commercial, social and religious, administrative, judicial and legislative affairs. The chief social obligations were education, health, thoroughfare, sanitation, water supply, maintenance of public institutions and many emergency measures during the time of famine. Each of these functions were exercised in accordance with definite rules and usages, some of them unwritten, others embodied in written agreements of charters as between the state and the panchayat or between the panchayat and its members. The village organization thus functioned in ancient times as a centre of community life and used to discharge even such functions as related to internal defence, and security, independently of the state which followed a policy of non–interference so long as it received its share of land revenue.

In olden days every village was a Republic. These were not based on legislative enactments but were custom based and traditional bound institutions. These institutions were sustained by a reciprocity of interests between landowners bound together by ties of kinship on one hand and the farm tillers and labourers on the other. The village governing was done by Panchayat or village council. The expression of villages selected for the purpose of village administration included the administration of justice. The word 'panchayat' indicates the number of those who originally constituted the council was fix. Word connotation analysis mean Panch and Ayat. Panch devotes institution and number of person who constitute the village council for performing administrative and judicial function. While Ayat is geometrical term and in English it is termed as rectangular means rectangular in shape.

In Vedic period, where rural administration was the main focus because urbanization had no place, the Panchayats were performing administrative and judicial functions. In *Manu* Sanhita, the relationship between king and village are described. It is also evident in Kautilya's *Arthashashtra* that state least interfere in rural administration. After the British rule, the role of Panchayats as institutions administering justice was abolished and replaced by legislation in 1860 such as the Indian Penal Code (IPC), Criminal Procedure Code (Cr. P.C.), Contract Act etc., along with land revenue settlements. These new laws supplemented the customary or traditional law. Collectorates and courts took over the powers of caste, village Panchayats to establish rule of law.

Panchayati Raj in Pre–Independence Period

In the early stages of British rule, the demand for democratic decentralization came from the elites who wanted share in the power and patronage. It was envisaged that the local bodies and municipalities must meet their local needs through local taxation. This principle was incorporated by Lord Mayo in a decentralization scheme formulated by the government in 1870 which made provision for taxes being raised locally by municipal and rural bodies to meet their local needs. The objective of Lord Mayo's scheme was to relieve the finances of British raj from management of local needs. Further, Lord Ripon extended a decentralized system of finance by transferring certain items of finances from the centre to local and municipal taxation to enhance their financial position and for uniform development throughout the country. Lord Ripon's Resolution of 1880 stressed the need of training elected representatives in particular and the people in general. The educative principle of training of people to participate in representative institutions of government should not be subordinated to demands for development activities. The budgetary freedom for development functions which was to be performed by local bodies was stressed upon. Finally, Lord Ripon's famous Resolution that came in 1882 has been regarded as the Magna Carta of Local Self–Government in

India and also known as father of local self–government in India. His emphasis was mainly on the political and popular training of educated Indians through these local representative institutions. The resolution categorically stated that the measure was chiefly designed as an instrument of political and popular education and utilize the rapidly growing class of intelligent and public spirited men. This helped in creation of numerous rural local boards in all states. The Bengal Municipal Act of 1884 and Bengal Local Self–Government Act, 1885 were formed by this philosophy. On 28th April 1915, through a resolution Government of India suggested gradual implementation of Lord Ripon's recommendations.

In 1919, Government of India introduced an Act of dyarchical system of local self governance through Montague–Chelmsford Reforms. In order to bring local supervision and monitoring of development activities, local bodies were constituted under the new Act. The taluka/tehsil served as basic unit for local boards and were responsible for sanitation, education and health services. These local bodies were also given powers to collect taxes. Under the Government of India Act, 1935, the provincial governments enacted legislations on local self government. The local government Acts were passed by the provincial governments to devolve powers of local development and administration upon Panchayats. All these provided for Panchayats by and large coterminus with administrative units like Patwari circle, tehsil/taluka and district. But the provincial governments jealously guarded their interests by providing powers to the collector to supersede the decisions of apex local district bodies. Local self–government, being provincial subject no taxes were earmarked for local bodies. But due to IInd World War in 1939, the municipal bodies instead of providing civic amenities functions were busy performing other functions. The functions were relating to practices in Black-outs, raising voluntary organizations for defence, increasing first aid etc., under the guidance and direct supervision of the district magistrate (DM).

Post Independence Period

After independence on August 15, 1947, the new Constitution of India declared it a Sovereign, Democratic Republic which came into force on 26th January 1950. At the time of formation of the Constitution, initially the inclusion of Panchayats was not considered in first draft, in the context of historical caste and class dominated structure in the villages. But it was modified during the discussion in the Constituent Assembly. And so a provision was included in Part IV of the Constitution (in the Directive Principles of State Policy) which is not mandatory. Article 40 reads "The state should take steps to organize village panchayats and endow them with such power and authority as may be necessary to enable them to function as units of self–government". Also, in the Constitution, 'local government' is mentioned in Schedule Seven, List II (State List) item which reads 'Local government that is to say the constitution and power of municipal corporation, improvement trust, district boards, mining settlement authorities and other local authorities for the purpose of local self–government or village administration'. Thus, it may be inferred that the Panchayats role was envisaged from the consideration of taking democracy to the villages and bringing powers to the village. Gandhiji considered the Panchayats to meet the village needs, and they focused on democratic decentralization and for devolving power upon people. However, Ambedkar expressed concern about the caste–ridden village society in India that had been detrimental to millions of people of weaker sections and he was very much for the concept of giving power to people.

While distributing powers between the Union and States, the Constitution of India Article 40 (Directive Principle of State Policy), vested local bodies and Panchayatiraj as a subject with states. Since independence, states have taken various measures for establishing Panchayati Raj System. There have been cases of success and failures. In this context, in order to examine the role and function of Panchayati Raj Institutions in development, various committees and experts groups were constituted.

In India, planning was introduced for the first time on Soviet Top–Down Model. The Central Government developed its own methodology and infrastructure for formulation of plans and development schemes and the states were required to follow and to execute the central programmes. They had no independent authority to decide their objectives and to draw their needs and priorities. Their main purpose was to secure the largest amount of grants from the Centre and they became gradually more and more dependent on Central assistance and less interested in the mobilization of their own revenues and resources. The first five year plan was launched in 1952 with a view to reducing poverty in rural India and introducing people's participation in the development programmes. Community Development Programmes was launched in First Five Year Plan in 1952 by creating 55 development blocks throughout the country which increased to 1075 at the end of first five year plan. The Community Development Programme was a method of rural development based on people's participation which sought to initiate the process of democratic decentralization for the transformation of the social and economic life of the villages in a coordinated and planned way.

Right from the beginning of the programme, participation of the people not only in the execution of the programmes but also in the formulation of schemes was stressed, and accordingly provisions for the setting up of a Project Advisory Committee as the representative of all the non–official elements within the project areas was visualized. But people's participation in the development process was sought to be achieved through an agent engaged in rural work, customarily described as the Village Level Worker (VLW). The first five year plan itself accepted the principle of democratic planning in which the people's co–operation was solicited in the implementation of the plan programmes. The plan document emphasized not only the vital role of the State Governments, but also of the Local Self governing bodies in the field of development. Different local, regional and functional bodies were required to be involved actively in the preparation of plans and the Central planning authority was visualized to be the preparation of general frameworks of the plan. Thus, the concept of decentralized planning became an important aspect of the successive five year plans. To assess and evaluate the Community Development Projects and National Extension Service, the Balwant Rai Mehta Committee was set up. The review of progress which followed during the Community Development era opened the eyes of the planners.

The Balwant Rai Mehta Committee made vital recommendations. The committee emphasized that community development would only be effective when the community was involved in the planning, decision and implementation process. Community development can be real only when community understands its problems, realizes its responsibilities, exercises the necessary powers through its chosen representatives and maintains a constant and intelligent vigilance on local administration. With this objective, the committee recommended an early establishment of statutory bodies and devolution upon them of necessary resources, power and authority. The report underlined the role of elected Panchayat Samitis at the community development block/tehsil level as the basic unit of democratic decentralization. The advisory role was contemplated for the Zila Parishads. The committee also focussed on rural sector and recommended that the functions of Panchayati Raj Institutions should cover the development of agriculture in all its aspects and the promotion of local industries and other services such as drinking water, road building etc. The tenure of Panchayat Samiti should be five years. The Panchayat Samiti had two sets of officers i.e. those at the block level and those at the village level. All of these officers were drawn from the corresponding state cadres and will be sent to the Panchayat Samiti by the state government.

The Panchayati Raj Institution was introduced in most parts of the country as a result of the Balwant Rai Mehta Report. However, the legislation that followed the Committee's Report basically continued the three tier structure and provided for overriding powers of the state government through the District Collector. These considerations were taken into account in the formulation of the Second Five Year Plan. Thus, the methods adopted for the preparation of Second Five Year Plan have provided valuable linkages between the village people and rural officials. The Second Five Year Plan stressed the need for creating effective administrative and development institutions at the base level for decentralized planning and rural development : "Unless there is a comprehensive village planning which takes into account the needs of the entire community, the weaker sections like tenants, cultivators, landless workers and village artisans may not benefit sufficiently from assistance provided by the government". Secondly rural progress depends entirely upon the existence of an active organization in the villages which can approach each family and bring all the people including the weaker sections of the community into production and other programmes to be carried out with the help of administration.

The Second Five Year Plan emphasized the need of district planning including the planning for blocks and groups of village and municipal areas. The need for creating a well organized structure of administration at district and below was also felt. But no concrete progress in this direction could be traced during the Second Plan period. The practice followed hitherto in planning and development remained almost the same during this period although the Second Five Year Plan discussed the concept and the scope of decentralized horizontal plans in great details. The Second Five Year Plan put much emphasis on district development administration especially on the models on which District Development Council were proposed to be built up in future. Thus, the district development administration was considered as an agency of change towards a new social order to respond to the needs and aspiration of the people. In the Third Five Year Plan, a new addition to the field of rural administrative machinery was added which paved considerable amount to decentralized planning and identified district level programmes. During the third plan, attempts were made to formulate state plans taking the district plans into account.

In 1963, another committee was set up to examine the issues of Panchayati Raj Institution finances in the name of K. Santhanam Committee. It was followed by Mehta Committee. Santhanam Committee recommendations covered a wide range of issues, the prominent among them were : the Panchayats should have more items that can be brought under tax net; the grants from the state level should be in the nature of united; and a Panchayat Raj Finance Corporation should be set up which would look into the financial resources of PRIs at all three levels, provide loans and financial assistance to these local institutions.

Since 1957, the functioning of the Panchayati Raj Institutions was marked with various shortcomings and the desired results could not be achieved. The people's participation in the activities of PRIs was limited. They did not identify themselves with these institutions and even Panchayats did not make attempts to ensure their involvement in decision making process. Many Panchayats were superseded and elections were not held for many years. Rather the whole process of development through Panchayats gave an opportunity to the rural elites to emerge as centre of power, and there usually was an alliance between local representatives and government functionaries at local levels. It further discouraged the rural poor and disadvantaged groups for meaningful participation in the decision making and implementation process. Also, the state government and the local political elites did not make positive steps to strengthen the local institutions.

Apart from above, as the funding for community development projects reduced considerably by the mid–1960s, Panchayats did not get enough funds for local development. They remained financially weak for decades without funds, superseded by decisions of district collectors, without elections being held to reconstitute them and could not provide representation for women, scheduled castes and tribes.

During the sixties, the economic atmosphere changed drastically. There was also speedy change in the political scenario after the fourth General Elections (1967). This changed political situation coupled with the economic uncertainty necessitated rethinking and reorientations of the development and planning policies. Certain progressive measures like Abolition of Privy Purses and the Nationalization of fourteen Commercial banks were undertaken by the government. Pursuant to this attitude of the government at the Centre, the Fourth Five Year Plan laid more emphasis on social justice and equity as well as on the solution of the problems of the weaker sections of the society. The real breakthrough in the sphere of planning process was made during the Fourth Five Year Plan period where planning system was decentralized by the Planning Commission. This paradigm of development was shifted by the think tank of the then Deputy Chairman of the Planning Commission D.R. Gadgil who popularized the concept of district plan. Gadgil developed his own ideas based on Puritan ethic principle and inspired by Japanese success, he wanted to make the planning to fulfill its role effectively. His methodology of district planning was based on two primary requirements : first being the knowledge regarding local conditions and the second was the participation of local people in the formulation and implementation of the plans.

During fifties and sixties, the planners and politicians had reduced the size of the unit of planning from the nation and state levels to the district and block levels, but the real question remained unsettled. In all these plans, 'people' were missing. The planners were perhaps confused. They could not settle the vital question : planning for whom ? The whole concept of decentralized planning appeared to be confused in a perception of getting the plans formulated for the people instead of planning by the people. But a decentralized plan is not produced by administrative decentralization only (for instance, by making state, district or even village level of administration responsible for implementing or even drawing the plans related to the geographical territory covered by them). In the absence of involving primary units of production in all aspects of planning, there is no decentralized planning. Indian planners believed that with the help of the state bureaucracy they would be able to achieve the targets. But the state apparatus which was modeled on the heritage and tradition inherited from the British raj, was not well suited for the task of rural reconstruction and development, in a country so vast and heterogenous like India. Indian bureaucracy, developed and nourished under the highly centralized steel frame of British administration, was turned into a district class which preferred to live in a narrow, circumscribed world of its own. The bureaucracy with its narrow horizon and exclusiveness fails to reach the masses, not to talk of influencing the way of life of the rural people. Virtually, a different kind of development machinery was required which could be entrusted with the responsibilities of planning and development.

It was the Fourth Five Year plan which spelt out the first time concrete steps in the direction of multi–level planning with the district as the main focus in the process and thereby it marked a watershed in the history of Indian planning. From the Fourth Plan onwards necessary steps were proposed to actualize decentralized planning. Later on, the Central Government initiated a scheme for financial assistance to the states for meeting additional expenditure for strengthening and reorganizing the state machinery. Now a concept of decentralized district planning became a development strategy. This necessitated the creation of an infrastructure and an effective change in the attitudes of the bureaucrats and politicians for the success of decentralized planning. Though both fourth and fifth five year plans were directed towards decentralization taking district and the block as the macro–levels of planning to speed up the works of planned rural development. But it was not translated into action. For the first time an attempt was made to treat the village as the lowest unit of decentralized planning by adopting the scheme 'Antyodaya' (whole village development programme) in 1977 in order to bring about the integrated development of the village as a whole. Real thrust on decentralized planning was given in the late seventies when the surplus production in wheat induced the Central Government to undertake new programmes like 'food for work' to combat rural poverty.

During the period of national emergency, bureaucracy got the upper hand and Panchayati Raj institutions lost much of their vitality and significance. National emergency ended in 1977 and the Janta Party swept the Lok Sabha polls. Decentralization of power and authority had been one of the plans of Janta Party during Lok Sabha election. It was observed by several state level committees and regional studies that Panchayati Raj system was suffering from a number of weaknesses. The central government appointed a high level committee on Panchayati Raj Institutions in 1977 under the chairmanship of Ashok Mehta and Working Group on Block Level Planning headed by M.L. Dantwala respectively. The Dantwala Committee was required to address the question of appropriateness of a block as a unit of planning and it recommended the case for selecting a small area for planning. However, in view of infrastructural difficulties at the block level, the committee assigned the responsibility of block planning to the district–level organization and suggested slow movement towards introduction of effective block planning. The committee proposed the integration of block plans with the district plan and thus the committee reviewed the preparation of both block and district plans to be a part of the same exercise.

To strengthen the Panchayati Raj Institutions, the Ashok Mehta Committee made some recommendations. This committee recommended grouping of a number of villages to constitute a Mandal Panchayat covering a population of 15,000 to 20000 for keeping the balance between technological requirements and possibilities for meaningful participation by the people. It would ensure administrative and economic viability and also facilitate the necessary linkages with the villages and gram panchayats. The committee suggested that the Block Level Panchayat Samitis would become non–statutory executive committees of Zila Parishads, and the Mandal Panchayats would carry out the development programmes. In the elections, the scheduled castes and scheduled tribes should get representation on the basis of their population. Panchayati Raj Institutions should be empowered with the powers to take their own decisions and prepare plans according to the local needs.

The recommendations of Ashok Mehta Committee opened a new era in local government and decentralized planning in India. The decentralized district planning and role of people's representatives in local bodies were considered basically to strengthen the process of development planning and democracy. However, the Sixth Five Year Plan sought to accommodate the recommendations of these committees and adopted the strategy to strengthen the process of democratic decentralization. Different poverty alleviation programmes like the Food for Work, the National Rural Employment Programme, Drought Prone Area Projects, Integrated Rural Development and the Rural Landless Employment Guarantee Programme etc., were introduced in the Central budget and a beginning in effective decentralization was made to ensure the planning and implementation in an effective and integrated manner, there was a need of an appropriate infrastructural machinery for launching above development programmes country wide. The Planning Commission appointed a working group on District Planning in 1982 under the Chairmanship of C.H. Hanumantha Rao and the recommendations of this group formed the basis for evolving the district planning and the approach was outlined in the Seventh Five Year Plan. The recommendations of the Working Group was incorporated in Seventh Five Year Plan and stated to pursue the decentralization of the planning process for development. It was also realized that planning activities at the district level would rest in a single district planning body which would determine the strategies and priorities and allocate funds for various departments taking into account the planning and other capabilities available at the grass root level. The development strategy of the Seventh Five Year Plan aims at the direct attack of the problems of poverty, unemployment and regional imbalances. The success of this depends on effective steps for the decentralization of planning and development administration, on one hand and involvement and participation of people in the formulation and implementation process through elected grass roots level institutions and voluntary agencies as well as organization of the poor on the other.

The idea of decentralized planning got a further fillip in the recommendations of the Commission on Centre–State Relations popularly known as the Sarkaria Commission and the Committee to Review the Existing Administrative Arrangements for Rural Development and Poverty Alleviation Programmes (CAARD) headed by G.K.V. Rao in 1985. The purpose of appointing Sarkaria Commission was mainly to examine and review the arrangements between the centre and the state. It provided a scope for strengthening the idea of regional planning in its recommendations on the issues like greater role for the State Planning Committees and the reorganization of National Development Council. While G.V.K. Rao Committee was constituted to examine various aspects of Panchayati Raj Institutions. After evaluating the functioning of local bodies, the committee made some important observations. It suggested for integrated rural development. It has to encompass all economic and social development activities handled by different agencies as field level. Panchayati Raj Institutions should be activated and given the necessary support so that they can become effective organizations for handling local development. Elections of local bodies should be held regularly. The Block Development Officer should be given pivotal role in the rural development process. But the district should be basic unit for policy planning and programmes implementation. And there is need to restructure the planning and implementation machinery.

In 1986, another committee was constituted by the Department of Rural Development, Government of India. The chairperson of the Committee was L.M. Singhvi, so it is also termed as Singhvi Committee which made some important recommendations in the field of Panchayati Raj Institutions. The committee considered the constitution of gram sabha for encouraging democracy at the grass root level. It recommended that the Panchayati Raj Institutions have to be viewed as institutions of self–government which would naturally facilitate the participation of the people in the process of planning and development and as a part of self–government. The committee envisaged and recommended that the Panchayati Raj bodies should be constitutionally recognized.

In the ultimate analysis, the way in which planning had been administered had left the people as mere spectator rathers than active participants in the entire process. Hence, the need for institutionalization of the process of decentralization to check the process of alienation of the people was felt.

Accordingly, the Eighth Five Year Plan laid down the emphasis on institution building to make the people's initiative and participation a key element in the process of development. The Eighth Plan stressed the role of government to facilitate the process of people's participation through the creation of necessary institutional infrastructure, particularly in the rural areas. But the progress was slow due to the fact that the other tiers of the government were not fully integrated into the development strategy. A review of the planning process provides enough indication that the Eighth Plan itself was involved in an experiment in district planning through the importance of decentralization.

Besides this neglected state of affairs in the process of decentralized planning, the overall progress in effective decentralization through Panchayati Raj was not at all satisfactory except in a few states. Rather the signs of instability and concentration of power became more visible in the process. There was a growing realization that the ineffectiveness and non–functioning of rural self–governing bodies was due to the result of the absence of constitutional recognition to the Pachayati Raj Institutions. This was states in the Ashok Mehta Committee and further gained ground in the reports of the Thungton Committee which recommended constitutional status for these bodies. The Thungton Committee (1988 which was) a sub–committee of the Consultative attached to the Ministry of Personnel also made exhaustive recommendations. Though constitutional status of Panchayati Raj Institutions was opposed by Sarkaria Commission, but the idea gained momentum in the late 1980s and was recognized in the 64th Constitutional Amendment Bill in 1989.

73rd Amendment Act and its Implications

In conformity with changing praxis of development theory, it is now realized and avowed that development of rural India can be concrete only through the process of decentralized planning and its implementation fully involving the people concerned. Consequently, to make the Panchayat as living, vibrant, "centre pillar of common wealth" the Constitution has been amended.

The 73rd Amendment Act by inserting a new part (Part XI) in the constitution enshrines continuity and strength to panchayat, directs the state governments to legislate and accordingly constitute panchayats by conferring powers and responsibility necessary to enable them to be evolved as self–governing institutions. And all these within the stipulated date of April 24, 1994. The Act is supposed to have ushered in a new era by making "genuine departure from the hitherto development orientation and reiterating that PRIs would be nothing short of self government institutions".

Panchayat Raj will now have uniform tier structure at village, intermediate (block) and district levels. However, the states having population below 20 lakh may dispense with tier at block level. Every Panchayat shall have fixed term of five years and elections to constitute new bodies shall be completed before the expiry of the term. In the case of earlier dissolution, elections have compulsorily to be held within six months. Seats in every Panchayats shall be filled by direct elections to be conducted by state election commission. In addition, the Chairperson of lower tiers will be ex–officio members of the succeeding tiers. The Member of Parliament (MP), Member of Legislative Assembly (MLA) may similarly be members of Panchayats of the concerned constituencies. Seats to be filled by direct elections in each Panchayat institutions have to be so distributed so as to conform, as far as practicable, to the ratio of population and number of seats throughout the state. Seats will have to be reserved for Scheduled Caste (SC) and Scheduled Tribes (ST) in proportion to their population in the Panchayat area and state. Posts of Chairperson in each institution shall be reserved in favour of SC, STs in proportion to their population in the area and state. Not less than one third of total seats to be filled by direct elections including similar proportion among those seats reserved for SC, STs and executive posts be reserved for women exclusively.

All reserved seats for SC, ST and women shall have to be allocated by rotation. State may therefore, reserve seats for Other Backward Classes (OBCs).

According to Article 243(G) of the 73rd Amendment : states will have to endow Panchayats with such powers and authority necessary for enabling them to function as institutions of self–government. States have been instructed to devolve power and responsibilities for capacitating them in:

1. Preparation of plans for economic development and social justice.
2. Implementation of schemes for economic development and social justice.

The Act also enjoins that PRIs will have adequate funds for carrying out functions and responsibilities and states will have necessary grants, assign revenues of certain taxes and authorize them to collect and retain a portion of revenue that they will raise.

India is now on the threshold of historic transition of political and economic process to the grass roots. All the central directives not withstanding, much depend upon the gestures of the State Government. Undoubtedly states and union territories have refurbished their Panchayat Acts largely in conformity with the constitutional prescription though all of them have preferred amendments instead of framing new acts altogether. With the constitution and consequent PR elections, the structural part has perceptively been fructified where the deviation and dithering glaring in earlier times has largely been arrested even though, for sure, not completely. While in pre-1993 period, the existence of PR entirely depended on the whim and caprices of states. The situation has improved unmistakebly. Though some may feel uncomfortable at the possibility of dissolution of these bodies but the mandate the re–constitution has to be made within six months time that makes the probability of abnegating Panchayat bodies somewhat moderate, if not nearly nugatory.

The Act has apparently opened the door to consequential changes in social, political, economic and administrative structures. By integrating SC, STs and women in the political process of Panchayats and by reserving executive post for these communities/groups as well as the voice and concerns of the under–represented and down trodden sections of rural society have given a chance to be counted. But inspite of the proclamation that PR would henceforth be self governing institution, how and where these bodies will have power and responsibilities is the moot question. Whether requisite entitlement and autonomy required for their evolving into self governing institutions as has been designated in the Central Act has factually been provided by any state Panchayat acts still is one contentious issue. Given the gestures of state government, whether the constitutional provision can effectively substitute the lack of political will is as yet dubious. Suffice, it to say that though the entity of PRIs has been secured, in the present context of operational autonomy, not much breakthrough is manifested and panchayats have not been able to shrug off their role solely as development agency.

In India travesty is that inspite of all support to the case of local level democracy and decentralization but none have really been able to translate into concrete practice. Despite the establishment of PRIs, meaningful decentralization of power, responsibility and financial devolution have persistently remained a day dream. The political will to make these bodies as real repository of authority like other strata of our political system is lacking. The ruling elites desist from breeding another set of power centre, they are in the main, obsessed by the fear psychosis and they tend to apprehend that it will pose direct threat to their authority, power and patronage. In the present backdrop, the polemic question is, whether and to what extent the new dispensation has really endowed and empowered rural local governments and whether they are fit enough for the nomenclature of self government. The point assumes still greater significance because as and even they actually become self government institutions the members to be elected there in will have wider scope in role performance, certainly more than that in the development agency.

The 73rd and 74th Constitutional Amendments in 1992–93 have ushered in the present phase where Panchayats are described as institutions of local self–government, and are expected to prepare plans for economic development and social justice. The Act stipulates some very vital measures for strengthening PR institutions, and besides constitutional status, the prominent among them are : time bound elections, powers to gram sabha, devolution of powers and funds, constitution of SFC, transfer of functions. There are now approximately 2,25,000 gram panchayats, 6,000 panchayat samitis and 550 zilla parishads duly elected and governed by state legislation in different states and union territories.

Salient Points of 73rd Constitutional Amendment Act, 1992

Constitutional status of Panchayati Raj System was a step in the direction of speeding up the process of decentralization and giving strength as well as stability to local institutions. In this perspective the need for conferring constitutional status to Panchayati Raj Institutions (PRIs) has validated the constitutional intention of Article 40, as envisaged at the time of formulation of Constitution.

The 73rd Constitution Amendment Act, 1992 came into force in 1993 with the assent of the President of India. The Act provides for the establishment of Panchayats in every state with the following features :

Gram Sabha : The Article 243A envisages for the constitution of gram sabha with the objective of providing participation to people in the decision–making process. The gram sabha means a body consisting of persons registered in the electoral rolls relating to a village comprised within the area of panchayat at the village level. The gram sabha may exercise such powers and perform such functions at the village level as the legislature of a state may by law provide.

Constitution of Panchayats : For having uniformity in the pattern of Panchayat structure, the Article 243B provides that there shall be constituted in every state, panchayats at the village level, intermediate and district levels in accordance with the provisions of this part. But for a low population state, notwithstanding anything in Clause (1), Panchayats at the intermediate level may not be constituted in a state having a population not exceeding 20 lakhs.

Composition of Panchayats : As per the Article 243C, the legislature of a state may, by law, make provisions with respect to the composition of Panchayats. As regards the representation in the Panchayat, it has been left to the state legislature to provide for the representation of:

- The chairperson of the Panchayats at the village level, in the Panchayats at the intermediate level.
- The chairperson of the Panchayats at the intermediate level, in the Panchayats at the district level.
- The members of the House of people and the members of the Legislative Assembly of the state.
- The members of the Council of States and the members of the Legislative Council of the state.

The chairperson and other members of a Panchayat whether or nor chosen by direct election from territorial constituencies in the Panchayat area shall have the right to vote in the meetings of the Panchayat. The act further provides that the chairperson of a Panchayat at the village level shall be elected in such a manner as the legislature of the state may, by law, provide and a Panchayat at the intermediate level or district level shall be elected by, and from amongst, the elected members thereof.

Reservation of Seats for Weaker Sections : In order to give representation to weaker sections in the Panchayats, the

Article 243D prescribes that the seats shall be reserved for the SCs and STs in every Panchayat and the number of seats so reserved shall bear, as nearly as may be, the same proportion to the total number of seats to be filled by direct election in that Panchayat as the population of the STs in that Panchayat area bears to the total population of that area and such seats may be allotted by rotation to different constituencies in a Panchayat. Not less than one–third of total number of seats reserved under Clause (I) shall be reserved for women belonging to the SCs and STs as the case may be.

Not less than one–third (including the number of seats reserved for women belonging to SCs and the STs) of the total number of seats to be filled by direct election in every Panchayat shall be reserved for women and such seats may be allotted by rotation to different constituencies in a Panchayat. The offices of the chairpersons in the Panchayat at the village or any other shall be reserved for the SC/STs and women in such a manner as the legislature of the state may provide by law.

The state legislatures can make provisions for reservation of seats in any Panchayat or offices of chairpersons in Panchayats at any level in favour of backward class of citizens.

Duration of Panchayat : In order to provide stability to the panchayats, the **Article** 243 E stipulates that every Panchayat, unless sooner dissolved under any law for the time being in force, shall continue for five years from the date appointed for its first meeting and no longer. No amendment of any law for the time being in force shall have the effect of causing dissolution of a Panchayat at any level.

Disqualification for Membership : The Article 243F has provided that a person shall be qualified for being chosen as and for being a member of Panchayat if he is so disqualified by or under any laws for the time being in force for the purpose of elections for the legislature of the state concerned, provided that no person shall be disqualified on the ground that he is less than 25 years of age, if he has attained the age of 21 years, if he is disqualified by or under any law made by the legislature of the state.

Powers, Authority and Responsibilities of Panchayats : In order to enable the panchayats to take up the task of preparation of plans for economic development and social justice, and the implementation of schemes for economic development and social justice, the legislature (as per Article 243G) of a state may, by law, endow the panchayats with such powers and authority as may be necessary to enable them to function as institution of self government.

Powers to Impose Taxes by and Fund of the Panchayats: Enhancing the own income of panchayats has been duly recognized by the Act, and so the Article 243H envisages that the legislature of a state may by law authorize a panchayat to levy, collect and appropriate such taxes, duties, tolls and fees in accordance with such procedure and subject to such limits. It may also make provisions for making such grants–in–aid to the Panchayats from the consolidated fund of the state.

Constitution of Finance Commission : The Article 243I envisages the constitution of State Finance Commission to review the financial position of the pancyhayats and to make recommendations as to the principles which should govern : (i) the distribution between the state and the panchayats of the net proceeds of the taxes, duties, tolls and fees levied by the state, (ii) the determination of the taxes, duties, tolls and fees which may be assigned to, or appropriated by the panchayats, and (iii) the grants–in–aid to the panchayats from the consolidated fund of the state, the measures needed to improve the financial position of the panchayats.

Audit of Accounts of Panchayats : As contained in the Article 243J, the legislature of a state may, by law, make provisions with respect to the maintenance of accounts by the panchayats and the auditing of such accounts.

Constitution of State Election Commission : for ensuring the fairness of the election process, as per Article 243K, State

Election Commission will look after the superintendence, direction and control of the preparation of electoral rolls for, and the conduct of, all elections to the panchayats. It also envisages that the legislature of a state may by law make provision with respect to all matters relating to, or in connection with, elections to the panchayats.

Application to Union Territories : The provisions of this part shall apply to the Union Territories and shall, in their application to a Union Territory, have effect as if the references to the Governor of a state were references to the administrator of the Union Territory appointed under Article 239 and references to the Legislature or the Legislative Assembly of a State were references, in relation to a Union Territory having a Legislative Assembly, to that Legislative Assembly. The President may, by public notification, direct that the provisions of this part shall apply to any Union Territory or part thereof subject to such exceptions and modifications as he may specify in the notification.

Part not to Apply to Certain Areas : The Article 243M stipulates that nothing in this part shall apply to the Scheduled Areas and the tribal areas, the states of Nagaland, Meghalaya and Mizoram, the hill areas of the state of Manipur for which District Councils exist under any law for the time being in force.

The Act further stipulates that nothing in this part relating to panchayats at the district level shall apply to the hill areas of the District of Darjeeling in the state of West Bengal for which Darjeeling Gorkha Hill Council exists under any law for the time being in force.

However, Parliament may, by law, extend the provisions of this part to the Scheduled Areas and the tribal areas referred to in Clause (I), subject to such exceptions and modifications as may be specified in such law, and no such law shall be deemed to be an amendment of this Constitution for the purpose of Article 368.

Bar to Interference by Courts in Electoral Matters : The Article 343O provides for the bar to interference by courts in electoral matters for certain specific matters concerning and the conduct of election. It lays down that notwithstanding anything in this Constitution : (a) the validity of any law relating to the delimitation of constituencies or the allotment of state to such constituencies made or purporting to be made under Article 243K, shall not be called in question in any court, and (b) no election to any panchayat shall be called in question except by an election petition presented to such authority and in such manner as is provided for by or under any law made by the legislature of a state.

Amendment of Article 280 : It prescribes that in Clause (3) of the Article 280 of the constitution, after sub–clause (b) the following sub–clause shall be inserted namely : (bb) the measures needed to augment the consolidated fund of a state to supplement the resources of panchayats in the state on the basis of the recommendations made by the Finance Commission of the state.

The Ninth Five Year Plan gave due emphasis on decentralized district planning but the final outcome is yet to be assessed. It envisaged a people–oriented planning in which not only the involvement of the Central and the State governments but also the people at large. It emphasized the transfer of adequate powers and authority to the panchayats so as to enable them to function as institutions of self–governance as visualized in the Constitution. The recommendations of the National Development Council for devolution of 41 percent of plan allocation to decentralized district planning were accepted but the extent of actual devolution of resources is yet to be ascertained. Though the plan sought to realize people's involvement in the decentralized planning through their elected representatives in order to evolve 'shared vision' of development towards common purpose. It is widely viewed that Ninth Plan failed to dovetail multi–level planning with multi–level public finance.

The 73rd and 74th Constitutional Amendments that conferred statutory status on PRIs and urban local bodies did not have only democratic decentralization as their objective. These institutions were also seen as a process for harnessing and channelizing the people's innate abilities to bring about rural transformation in a way that every individual acquired his/her rightful place in the social, economic and political arena.

The Ninth Five Year Plan had called for the devolution of the functional responsibilities dealing with subjects listed in the Eleventh Schedule of the Constitution and financial resources for taking up development programmes to the PRIs. There have been mixed progress on this front. Political devolution has taken place. Elections have been held and women, SC/STs and other marginalized groups have got political representation in the rural areas. Problems encountered in the process of evolution of Panchayats has been taken care of with the intervention of courts, civil society organizations and increased public awareness. The strengthening of forces that facilitate political empowerment of rural communities would be an important area of action in the Five Year Plan period. Issues of the transparency, accountability and development would require greater attention. States which have lagged behind in devolving functions and finances to panchayats would have to be encouraged to empower the panchayats.

The gram sabhas in most of the states have been entrusted with only ceremonial functions. The power and functions of gram sabhas need to be enlarged by giving them effective power of implementation and monitoring of development plans. Social audit of all development programmes by gram sabha would be made mandatory. The committee system adopted in many states to facilitate a more participative decision making process in the panchayats should be incorporated in the State Panchayat Acts. The powers entrusted to a gram sabha in a Scheduled V area could be extended to gram sabhas in non–scheduled areas as well.

Administrative and financial devolution by the states to the PRIs remain an area of major concern. The constitution has placed onerous responsibilities of PRIs. They require financial resources to discharge the tasks assigned to them and emerge as viable institutions of self government. Financial devolution is also desirable as the control of investment decisions by local committees leads to better utilization of scarce resources. Panchayats would need greater powers of taxation and avenues for non–tax revenue. States could provide matching grants to panchayats to takeup specific projects. Apart from the funds that flow to panchayats for centrally sponsored and state sector schemes, untied grants could also be provided to the PRIs.

The onus for devolving functions, functionaries and financial resources to the PRIs rests with the state governments. Though the states have slowly transferred functions and finances to the PRIs, these institutions are hampered by lack of administrative support. PRIs have to be adequately staffed and the functionaries must be trained in planning, budgeting and accounting tasks. An elaborate system for auditing of panchayat finances has to be put in place. At present, adequate safeguards against the misuse of resources by elected functionaries do not exist in many states. These issues need to be tackled on a priority basis.

The 74th Constitution Amendment Act provided for the constitution of District Planning Committees (DPCs). However, the Constitutional provision of DPCs is rather weak as it provides for the preparation of only draft plans by the DPCs. State governments have not given adequate attention to the DPCs and the Government of India's guidelines on district planning have not been fully operationalized. DPCs should be set up and its functionaries must be trained in the basics of planning. The gram sabha/panchayat should be associated with the preparation of village development plan based on the felt needs of the people. These plans should be integrated with the panchayat samiti and district level plans to make the grass root planning process a reality in the Tenth Plan period.

As against a total expenditure of Rs. 35,866 crores in Ninth Plan the allocation for the Tenth Plan period has been increased to Rs. 56.748 crores to the scheme-wise breakup.

Enabling Political Empowerment : Panchayati Raj Institutions (PRIs).

Notable constitutional, legislative and policy reforms, and continued administrative decentralization have demonstrated the government's commitment to increase women's grass roots participation. Although, only one third of seats were reserved for women by the 73rd and 74th Constitutional Amendments, the actual representation is higher at all levels. Women's increased political participation has yielded a range of positive results, not only for women, but also for their families and communities. Central issues in development such as health, nutrition, family income and education are finding their way to the top of the agenda for action. Women participation brings about more inclusive governance and effective community–centred development. Yet in many places, especially in the states like U.P., Bihar and Rajasthan, women continue to serve as proxies. The challenge for the Eleventh Plan is to ensure that women panchayat members are empowered to take their own decisions.

Eleventh Plan will undertake the following measures to accelerate the process of women's political empowerment and participation in PRIs.

The no–confidence clause is often used to remove women Sarpanches. State governments will be advised to ensure that women Sarpanches cannot be removed for at least a year and half by no confidence motion. If a no–confidence vote is passed, the replacing incumbent should also be a woman from the same social group as the earlier incumbent; states should revisit the two–child norm that prevent those who have more than two children from holding office. This law has been repeated across some states because it was found to be used against women in that it disproportionately impacted poor, SC, ST, Muslim, and tribals. More tragically, the norm led to increasing female foeticide; Increase resource allocation for capacity building of all PRI members (male and female) in diverse areas pertaining to gender sensitization and women's rights, as well as in the political skill building of women members of PRIs; greater effort to include poor and other excluded women on State Planning Boards and Commissions; Funds for time–series evaluations of the impact of women on PRIs, and on enabling on policy conditions and contextual factors for women's political participation; accelerate the state government's process of devolution and decentralization of powers, so that PRIs are not handicapped in carrying out their mandated duties.

The significance of this multilevel planning process is not yet understood in its entity. The introduction of decentralized district planning calls for a new ecological setting and a new culture in planning and decentralization radically different from First Five Year Plan upto Eleventh Five Year Plan. However, the new experiments have already been started to attain the development goals through popular democratic setup. All the states have passed the State Conformity Acts and have incorporated the constitutional changes in their respective state laws. In most of the states, District Planning Committees have been constituted for undertaking decentralized district planning. But these changes necessitate a determined and sustained effort for introducing multilevel federalism in administration under less bureaucratic control. Constitutional amendments have created the necessary structure for decentralized planning and new conditions are required for implementing the schemes and strengthening the process of decentralized district planning in its actual practice.

In order to examine the problems of women representatives in Decentralized Governance and Panchayati Raj we have conducted a research study. 73rd Amendment Act of the Constitution which came into force from April 24, 1993 has proposed not less than one–third of the total number of seats to be filled by direct elections in every panchayat to be reserved for women. This gender based reservation policy in favour of women is made applicable even to the number of seats otherwise reserved for scheduled castes, and scheduled tribes and other backward classes of women in all three tiers of Panchayati Raj Institutions. Provisions have also been made that not less than one–third of the total member of offices of Chairperson and members in the Panchayats at each level shall be reserved for women.

Objectives

The study was conducted keeping in mind the main objectives which are listed below :

1. To study emerging perspectives, issues, trends and also paradigm shifts in rural development, decentralized governance and Panchayati Raj Institutions in India;
2. To study socio–economic characterization of women Panchayat representatives and also to analyze women's participation in politics;
3. To study women's participation in Panchayati Raj Institutions at all levels, i.e. election, attending meetings and sharing power in terms of decision making;
4. To find out obstacles as well as socio–cultural factors which influence or create hindrance in effective participation of women in Panchayati Raj Institutions;
5. To study women's involvement in programming and management of developmental projects in their concerned area and their role in community development;
6. To examine problems, constraints, challenges and socio–cultural value system which creates hindrance to women representatives in political institutions as well as decentralized rural governance; and

7. Finally to suggest policy measures for empowerment of women; identify the critical areas of women's effective participation and involvement in development and social change.

Methodology

The nature of proposed study is an empirical research with quantitative approach and based on primary data collected through field study. In addition to this, secondary data and relevant literature has also been consulted. Universe of the study consists of two states, namely Uttar Pradesh and Chattisgarh. From each state, two districts are chosen, Gonda and Sitapur in Uttar Pradesh, Raipur and Bilaspur in Chhattisgarh respectively. For more comprehensive field study two blocks in every district and in every block, five village panchayats are selected.

2

Decentralization: Concept and Constitutional Provisions

The decades of 1950s and 1960s saw the demands (Kueck, et.al., 1998) coming from people and a number of civil society groups for a variety of development needs ranging from health to poverty alleviation to marketing of agricultural produce to civic amenities. The central governments in several countries felt the pressure for addressing these problems. Thus, it was a period that was marked with the setting up of local governments in a number of countries. A new thinking and approach on local governments that could meet the challenges of local development got favourable response. The expert writings (Maddick, 1970) further promoted and exemplified this trend. They dwelt at length on the needs and the limitations of decentralized system of government. The discussion focused on various forms of decentralization, planning, organizational structure and management of basic services.

The decade of 70s saw the emergence of decentralization as a development alternative, and got the focused attention when the debate picked up momentum in 1980s. Many countries in Asia and Africa emphasized the role of decentralization as a means of national development and for achieving a variety of development objectives, ranging from people's participation to meeting their aspirations to political stability. This period saw paradigm shift in the approach for development, and led to shift in orientation from structured development planning to planning from below and from growth to redistribution of income with the objectives of equality, improved quality of life and reduction in poverty.

Decentralization : Meaning and Development of the Concept

The term decentralization is understood differently by different individuals or groups. Louis A. Allen refers to it as one of the most confused and confusing of the administrative techniques that characterize the art and science of professional management. To quote Pfiffner and Sherwood, "In some respects, decentralization has come to be a gospel of management. Firstly it is regarded as a way of life to be adopted as least partially on faith; secondly it is an idealistic concept, with ethical roots in democracy, thirdly it is in the beginning a more difficult way of life because it involves a change in behaviour running counter to historically–rooted culture patterns of mankind. Men find it difficult to delegate, to think in terms of the abstractions required by long–term planning, to listen rather than give orders, to evaluate other men and their work in terms of overall results instead of irritations and tensions of the moment. Yet this is the very key to the behaviour required of leaders in a decentralized organization".

Decentralization has a spatial aspect. When a wide organization has its activities spread over a wide geographical space, planning and control of the widely dispersed activities may be done better from points away from the central headquarter. It is an illustration of Gullick's area principle in operation. A third argument in favour of decentralization revolves round the need for organization autonomy. A decentralized unit can function better when it is organized semi–autonomously without being subjected to detailed central control. Lastly, decentralization has been supported by the democratic argument that this arrangement facilitates lower level 'participation' in decision–making.

In organization theory, decentralization has been conceived basically as an aspect of intra–organizational differentiations. A complex, large–scale organization, meeting a dynamic 'task environment' seeks to adapt itself through segmentation and arrangement in self–sufficient clusters, each having its own domain. Decentralized divisions emerge as a consequence, which are sometimes called product divisions of profit centres.

Decentralization has also been approached from the point of view of organization decision–making. Organization complexity entails more numerous and quicker decisions to achieve efficiency. When speed assumes critical importance, decentralized decision–making is usually resorted to. It has been suggested that the degree of decentralization is greater under the following conditions :

(i) Greater number of decisions is made at lower levels of management;

(ii) Decisions made at lower levels are important;

(iii) Various organizational functions are more influenced by decisions made at lower levels.

(iv) There is less monitoring of decisions made by managerial personnel.

Organizational decentralization, thus conceived, manifest itself in territorial dispersion of units and delegation of authority. Field administration in the form of district and sub–divisional administration, for instance, represents decentralization through territorial differentiation and dispersion. It is an integral part of state administration. Its particularity lies in its physical location away from the state headquarters to provide access to the client. Delegation of authority has naturally to accompany territorial dispersion of the governmental unit.

Theoretical knowledge about decentralization in politics and organizational designing has been greatly advanced by Kochen and Deutsch in their seminar paper entitled "Toward a Rational Theory of Decentralization : Some Implications of a Mathematical Approach". A functional theory of decentralization, according to them, has to be related to organizational task performance and ultimate survival.

Organizations depend critically on the feedback of information from the environment in order to ascertain the results of their actions and to take corrective measures. The issue of centralization versus decentralization has to be examined from the point of view of exchange of information and of things and persons with the environment. Kochen and Deutsch thus look at decentralization as a problem in logistics. Decentralization is rational or cost–effective if movement of messages, men and materials and leads to successful task performance in relation to meeting the demands and pressures from the environment. To quote their observation "For a functional theory of decentralization, ... the social tasks to be performed are more important than the historical institutions which currently happen to perform them. Though institutions have a great deal of persistence and tend to protect their own survival, they nonetheless do change. Some of these changes tend toward greater or lesser decentralization, and a functional analysis of the level of decentralization most appropriate to their chief task is essential in order to evaluate rationally the actual changes which occur in response to technological or political pressures.

This formulation is palpably oriented towards operational effectiveness of organizations. It is valuable contribution to theoretical knowledge no doubt, but the weakness of such an instrumental approach lies in its exclusive emphasis on functionality alone. Decentralization has more than functional importance. It may reflect commitment to some kind of ethical and political value as well.

To return to organization theory, decentralization has generally been conceived as a means to organizational efficiency in limited circumstances of complexity and scale. Its essence has been deconcentration or decongestion of the headquarters unit.

In political science and public administration, decentralization has been discussed basically from the view point of arrangement of government. The different approaches to the concept have been clearly and profoundly presented by Fesler. Following his classification, the approaches can be grouped into four categories : the doctrinal, the political, the administrative and the dual–role.

The *doctrinal approach* seeks to treat decentralization as an end in itself through a process of 'romantic idealization'. The Gandhian concept of 'concentric circle' of power distribution and the idealization of village community in panchayati raj have reduced decentralization almost to a dogma and an article of faith. Instead of treating decentralization as a means to the achievement of some end values, such idealization tends to elevate it to the status of a hardened doctrine.

The *political approach* underscores the essentially political character of decentralization. Initiatives to decentralize, and willingness to pass on powers and functions to decentralized units, and to allow these units to actually operate within a framework of autonomy, are politically determined. Creation of field units of government, away from central headquarters, exemplifies deconcentration. Decentralization in the shape of devolution to local self–governing bodies marks an attempt to set up autonomous governments at the level of the locality. Field units of government like district administration are the long arms of the central (state) governments and do not pose problems of organizational discontinuity whereas local self–governing bodies that are elected locally to determine local policies and to implement them are, in a fundamental–way, detached from the central (state) government. To create and maintain local government is thus a major political commitment. In the absence of such commitment, devolution to sub–national governments, including local self–governing bodies, will remain more in law than in practice. This leads to what Fesler has called 'illusory decentralization'. Both panchayati raj and municipal government in India represent to a considerable extent this sort of façade devolution. Now, of course, with the passage of 73rd and 74th Constitutional Amendment Acts (1992), these local government institutions have been accorded a constitutional status with necessary powers and resources.

The *administrative approach* to decentralization is motivated by efficiency criterion. Enhancement of administrative rationality becomes the desideratum. When field administrative units are set up through a process of deconcentration, the measure is considered appropriate for field level decision making and prompt problem–solving. In this process, administrative units might come up at many levels between the locality and the central (state) headquarters. With more and more demand for specialized functions, multiplicity of functional departments would appear at the field level. The administrative situation gradually presents a picture of polarization between general area–based administrative demands and specific function–centred claims of particular functional departments. Currently, district administration in India is faced with this problem of area function duality. Decentralization in administrative terms may not therefore always guarantee 'clarity of authority and orderliness of operations'. To promote such operational principles conscious attempts are needed to readjust from time to time the conflicting claims of area and functions in deconcentrated field administration.

Finally, *the dual–role approach*, as Fesler puts it, is a kind of rehearsal of the area–function dichotomy in a new setting. Decentralization is placed within a larger context of development and change, as distinguished from maintenance of status quo. Conceived in administrative terms, the dual role approach seeks to highlight the conflict in field administration between tradition and change. Most field administrative systems were evolved in an earlier era mainly to maintain the established order, to collect revenue and to keep things from going wrong. Almost all the developing countries that have inherited the colonial field system are seeking to bring about speedy social and economic change. The functions of field administration have changed radically as a consequence. To quote Fesler, 'The intent is to change established ways of doing things so as to carry economic and social development forward rapidly. This contrasts with the status quo orientation of a field system geared to maintenance of the established order. Thus conflicting with the personal orientation of field generalists so chosen and trained as to identify themselves with the classes, families and other groups who constitute the 'establishment'. Resolution of conflict between two different orientations in field administration calls for adaptation of decentralization to changing circumstances. The theme is not unfamiliar to Indian administration in general and district administration in particular.

The latest thinking on decentralization veers around power equation and participation. Organization theory and political science which did not meet very often in the past have now almost come together in explicating the concept of decentralization concertedly. The concern in organization theory is increasingly about individual welfare which is considered feasible and desirable through participative management. In political science, decentralization reappears as a means to the achievement of a more participative democracy that goes beyond traditional electoral methods of intermittent representation.

The value being maximized via organization theory is individual employee's 'health'; whereas the value being maximized via political science is redistributive politics as a means to community and citizen oriented 'political health'.

Contemporary thinking on decentralization can be looked at from three angles. Firstly, it is thought of as a means to spiritual enrichment and growth of the individual both as worker and citizen. Decentralization offers opportunity to participate in decision making. For an individual, it is an aid to the growth and development of personality.

Secondly, decentralization has an instrumental value as a means of improving organizational performance. Public administration is related to the operational aspects of government. The operations are better done through decentralization which provides access to local information and data, and creates conditions for local popular support to administrative action. Administration is opened up in a decentralized system, as it no longer remains a secretive operation of proud specialists.

Thirdly, the current thinking, very importantly, reflects a paradigmatic shift in public administration as a discipline. The bureaucratic model which has so long dominated the field seems inadequate to explain the contemporary politico–administrative situation. As Thompson pointed out, the Weberian formulation has no concern for the client. As an inward–looking mechanistic construct, it has set up an organizational model without reference to the catchment area of the organization that determines its locus standi. The decentralization–participation debate introduces a new perspective in public administration and calls for its reconstruction.

It is amply clear that decentralization is not only a device for the delegation or dispersal of administrative authority, but it is also a democratic method of devolution of political authority. It is also an essential element to adopt the democratic norms. Such norms help the various levels of the administrative organization to develop a reasonable capability for the exercise of authority to reach the most desired decisions. Moreover, they help to assimilate in them the virtues of greater interactions not only among the various organizational levels but also between the organizations and the clientele among the general public.

It has been opined that decentralization refers to the physical location of facilities and the extent of dispersal of authority throughout an organization. Hence, it has an arrangement by which the ultimate authority to command and the ultimate responsibility for results is localized in units located in different parts of the country. It is argued that assigning of functions and responsibility, for their efficient and effective performance to the subordinates or subdivisions is the essence of decentralization. In a decentralized organization, lower levels are allowed to decide many matters and a few cases involving major policies or interpretations are referred to the higher levels of the organization. Decentralization covers the political, legal and administrative spheres of authority.

Steps of the Decentralization : The Constitutional Provisions

On Independence in 1947, India like many former British colonies, adopted model of British Parliamentary democracy along with its main features, such as accountability of the executive to the legislature, a professional military, a politically neutral career Civil service, and the rule of law, all operating within the framework of parliamentary supremacy. But some salient features of the political system of the United States such as Federalism, the separation of powers, and fundamental rights of individuals protected by Supreme Court were also introduced. The leaders of the downtrodden most notably Baba Sahib Bhim Rao Ambedkar under the overall leadership of Pt. Jawahar Lal Nehru wanted to give concrete shape to a broad vision of a modern, secular, democratic India, mobilizing its resources toward the twin objective of growth and redistribution.

The Separation and Division of Powers

Levels of Government	*Executives*	*Legislative*	*Judicial*
National	President–in–Council	Parliament	Supreme Court
Regional	Governor–in–Council	Assembly	High Court
Local	District Megistrate	Zila Parishad	District Court

One of the legacies of the Indian resistance to British rule was a deep distrust of power and determination to secure the maximum possible freedom for citizens. The Constituent Assembly, which met from 1947–1950, sought to give shape to these aspirations in the institutions they devised. In some political legacies, but in others they borrowed widely from the major constitutions of the western world. The result was the separation of power into the executive, the legislature and the judiciary, at the national level represented by the President and the Council of Ministers, the Parliament, and the Supreme Court respectively. There was an equally robust division of power between the federal government and the regions. In this enthusiasm for the decentralization of power, the constituent assembly did not stop there. Strong hopes were expressed for the further devolution of power below the level of the regional governments, to be exercised directly by the representatives of the people. This hope was given concrete shape in 1957, when the Balwant Rai Mehta Committee recommended the creation of Panchayatiraj, where representative bodies to be setup at the district, sub–district or block and villages level, and to be endowed with measure of administrative autonomy, charged with developmental functions and given financial means for the purpose. The phase of implementation of Panchayati Raj has been far from uniform in the country as a whole, but thanks to the Seventy Third Amendment of the Constitution, all of India's half million villages are covered by some form of direct exercise of power.

In directive principles of state policy, Article Forty (40) also ensures that "The state shall take steps to organize village panchayats and endow them with such powers and authority as may be necessary to enable them to function as units of self–government".

Federalism is a system in which political power is divided between Central (National) Government and smaller government units. The Central Government is often called the Federal Government, and the smaller units, States or Provinces.

Factors Leading to Decentralization: The Indian Context

- Historically many developing countries followed the system of central command and traditional control by elites, which flourished under the guise of patronage. With the time, degeneration of patronage system took place this played a vital role in opening up of opportunities for people to express their grievances, in building pressure.

- Many countries over–centralized power so much that it undermined the autonomy, resources, effectiveness and responsiveness of institutions. People at the lower level started becoming impatient with the failure of governments to deliver. The governments faced mounting demands from organized groups, which got compounded by the sluggish economic growth and increasing corruption by elites at all levels that undermined their ability to respond to the demands of various groups.
- Colonial period – not meeting people's aspirations. Several developing countries, that saw the central rule without giving regard to local problems and their needs, preferred to have decentralized development system in order to evolve the people in the development process and also to empower them.
- The industrial development in a decentralized way, which promoted flexible small units, also influenced the thinking. By the late 1970s, many industries taking technological advantages did well due to their flexible nature and their capacity to react quickly to changing conditions and consumer demands. Subsequently, in the developing countries the process of liberalization has contributed towards decentralized thinking. Likewise, the development also required to be responsive to people's need to address the problems in the fast socio–economic scenario. This drove the policy makers towards greater decentralization.
- During the 1980s, some donor agencies also began to shift their emphasis away from large scale development programmes to more small, micro–level

projects into which grass root communities could be drawn as participants, in the hope of making development more sustainable (Manor, 1980).

- The failure of decentralized institutions in the East European countries generated a favourable climate for decentralization in the developing world.
- The democratization of numerous formerly autocratic regimes, especially in Africa, led to thinking of more role for civil society, and that facilitated the creation of local government because of its proximity to people and for bridging the gap between the state and marginalized groups.
- Cultural factors like traditional role of village councils (or panchayats), community action, consensus approach and so on, have contributed towards decentralization. For instance, in the developing countries like India and Bangladesh, the functioning of village panchayats (since historical times) in the village affairs influenced the decision for establishing local government system.

Decentralization and the Indian Polity

It has been proved in the past that the centrally controlled national planning has severe limitations. The central planning systems have been unable to provide for equitable distribution of the benefits of economic growth among regions and groups within developing countries. It was realized that development, being a complex and uncertain process, can not be planned and controlled from the centre. The decision makers at the centre would not be able to understand the needs of heterogenous regions and groups.

When functions and authority are being transferred to the local levels, or to the persons concerned with the problems and needs, they take more interest in the work. It is the sense of participation in development planning and management that encourages them.

The central government officer's knowledge of local problems and needs can also be increased. They become more sensitive to various problems at the local level when they are being reassigned to local levels. When there is closer contact between government officials and the local population, better information can be obtained. And with better information more realistic and effective plans for projects and programmes can be formulated.

In central planning and management, there is over concentration of power, authority and resources at the centre. Thus, red–tape and highly structured procedures are its inevitable characteristics. The developing countries have to achieve development goals within a target period. It is decentralization which can cut through red–tape and highly structured procedures.

Decentralization can lead to the development of greater administrative capability among local governments, thus, expanding their capacities to take over functions that are not usually performed well by central ministries.

Decentralization can also provide a structure through which activities at various central government ministries and agencies involved in development could be coordinated more effectively with each other and with those of local leaders and non–governmental organizations within various regions.

Decentralization would lead to creation of alternative means of decision making. Thereby, the local elite who are unsympathetic to national development policies and insensitive to the needs of the poorer groups in rural communities, would not be able to have control over development activities.

Decentralization for Welfare and Development Concerns

Most countries have gone for decentralization with variety of goals in mind. Some of them have often proceeded on the basis of genuine considerations of empowering the people at the grass root level.

- Providing opportunities to people for their socio–economic development;
- Enhancing people's participation at lower levels by providing them opportunities in the decision–making;
- Utilizing the local knowledge in the development planning;
- Raising the competence level of development functionaries and the capacity of local institutions for more sustained development;
- By equitable distribution of resources;
- Empowering the weaker sections through improvement in their capabilities by giving them voice in the decision–making;
- Facilitating socio–economic development including alleviation of poverty by way of tapping individual potential and the services of social groups at local levels;
- Enhancing the transparency of functioning and responsiveness as well as accountability of departments, elected representatives and political institutions to people, and thus improving the efficiency of functioning; and
- Also providing opportunities to people at the lower level for future political role.

Objectives of Decentralization

Decentralization refers to a process of assigning the public functions and responsibilities of planning and implementation from central government to sub–district level in order to carry out specific tasks at the local level. As indicated by this definition, the public affairs are to be managed at the local level and there are certainly specific objectives for the need to choose the path of decentralization. The prominent among them are :

- Firstly, to handle promptly the local–specified development needs : there are functions, which have only or predominantly local significance, along with functions which depend substantially for their performance upon information and resources available locally, can be better managed by the local bodies. For example, community roads, local water supply, school and markets can be better handled by the local administration.

- Secondly, to improve the efficiency of programme implementation : considering the issues from the point of view of administrative efficiency, we need to divide up and disperse the workload to the organizations in the field to benefit from local knowledge for their efficient implementation. Decentralization of functions gives dividends in terms of speed and efficiency in service and performance. It helps in achieving better coordination of related functions assigned to a variety of local officers and it takes lesser time in taking decisions at the local level than the time taken in centralized planning system.
- Thirdly, to reach the distant locations effectively : through decentralization the benefits of development can be extended to people in distant localities more equitably and to meet the different needs of a diverse population.
- Fourthly, to increase the responsiveness of local administration to people's needs : the actions of local level development functionaries can be best monitored by the local population, and through their regular feedback, an effective control is possible, which will help in making the local administration more responsive.

Variants of Decentralization

The variants of decentralization are de–concentration, delegation, devolution and privatization. These are defined as :

De–concentration implies handing over limited central government powers, functions and resources to its field units.

Delegation implies transferring responsibility for specifically defined functions to lower level organizations.

Devolution implies transfer of functions and authority with a greater autonomy in respect to certain defined functions, including decision–making authority. The authority handed over to local institutions through devolution can be taken back only after making amendments in the law.

Privatization refers to a form of decentralization in which the government may transfer functions to voluntary organizations or private enterprises and allow them to perform certain functions.

Types of Decentralization

Decentralization has got many dimensions. These include political, functional, administrative, financial and geographical decentralization respectively. And the vital issues, under those dimensions, range from environment in the panchayat area to people's participation, to capabilities of panchayati raj members, to capacity of local institutions to deliver, to financial devolution, to fiscal management and to accountability. Under the present dispensation of decentralization, the states have to attend issues and to provide operational shape to decentralization process.

Now, in the context of the complex and multidimensional matter of decentralization system, a systematic methodology is required to reduce subjectivity in the analysis and bringing objectivity as much as possible (Saxena, 1995). The system approach offers one such possibility. System approach focuses an output and integrates the various administrative process in a logical way, or it can be defined as logical problem solving process, which is applied to identifying and resolving important development problems. The focal point of this approach is the 'system'. Here the system, is assumed to be having elements on parts which have dynamic relationships among themselves and with the whole, and each of these parts affect independently or in relation with other (one or more than one) influence the outcome.

In decentralization process, various components such as environmental building, capacity building, transfer of functions and devolution of funds, fiscal management, planning delivery mechanism and accountability are closely linked to each other and the one affects the outcome of the other.

Political Decentralization

Under political decentralization, people are drawn into decision making process through empowerment. Political or democratic decentralization thus signifies the quest for a participative and community approach. It entails the transfer of authority from central government to autonomous and local tiers that have been democratically elected by their constituencies.

Political decentralization involves that the political powers and functions concentrated in the hands of higher level political organs are decentralized to lower level political organs. Panchayati Raj agencies are units of decentralization wherein political powers decision making are decentralized from state governments to Panchayat Samitis and Zila Parishads. Election of local bodies in a free manner is a vital part in the process of decentralization. Issues that are crucial are fairness of election process, the external factors that influence the election, role of political parties etc. There are various problems like money and physical power, consumption of liquor etc., during the process of elections that effect outcome of the election. Also of significance is the representation of weaker sections of the society e.g. Scheduled Castes and Scheduled Tribes and Women in the panchayat bodies. Socio–political and cultural environment affects the working environment of panchayats. Good social relation among people and proper functional understanding among various groups will add to harmonious functioning while on the other hand, warring groups on divisions on party lines may vitiate the atmosphere of working at panchayat level. The cultural factors like caste (discriminations), role of village elites, decision–making process, prestige for winning elections, exercising control over village panchayat and role (in terms of importance given) of poor and other weaker sections in the panchayat functioning, influence the environment in the village.

Political status is important to ensure the functional autonomy of the local bodies and to give executive position to elected representatives. The people's participation in the decision making of village development planning and implementation is crucial and is one of the ultimate objectives of decentralization. It is measured in terms of participation by people in election, the category of people participating in the discussion, the response of Panchayati Raj members in the gram sabha, relationship of people with elected representatives, types of issues discussed in the gram sabha and mode of identification of works in the gram sabha and so on. And accountability requires the system or procedure of making elected representative responsible for their duties and answerable to people, and to ensure fairness in the panchayat functioning so that the decisions are taken on merit and the elected members take steps to rectify their improper or wrong decisions.

The size of the panchayats also assumes importance in order to enable them to deliver services to people keeping in view of physical reach and also from the point of view administrative and financial viability. Capacity of Panchayati Raj members is vital for their abilities to deliver. Here, the factors that are crucial are dummy candidates, no educational and financial background of Panchayati Raj members and their capabilities.

Responsiveness of Panchayati Raj members assumes high significance in the process of decentralization. It is one of the important factors that will determine how the panchayats will attend to people's grievances and their needs. It is measured by how Panchayati Raj members attend to the development priorities, how they address people's grievances at Gram Panchayat level and how they attend to the problems of weaker sections like landless people, women and poor. Representation of gram panchayats in higher tiers is important to assess how the gram panchayats are given role and voice in the decision–making process of higher tier. Also of importance is the role of MLAs and MPs in the functioning of panchayats.

Functional Decentralization

It implies that the functions are decentralized to the specialized units or departments like education, health, etc. It also refers to transferring subject specific functions to local tiers. The functions under 29 subjects, as identified in 11th Schedule are to be transferred to panchayats. Also, inter tier demarcation of functions for each subject is important in order to clearly specify the functions that are to be handled by particular tier.

Administrative Decentralization

It refers to decentralization of authority to the lower officials in the administrative hierarchy of organizations. It means decentralizing powers or functions to the subordinate units which involves placing planning and implementation responsibilities with the local bodies and assigning the roles and responsibilities to functionaries and elected members.

Participatory planning is important for eliciting people's knowledge about local problems, needs and resources during the process of planning so that the plans so prepared will reflect the people's needs and aspirations in a more meaningful way. Planning is important for rational allocation of resources at the local level. Planning methodology, people's participation, supporting unity at each tier and database preparation are vital for the success of participatory local level planning. Implementation of works should involve procedure for work execution, beneficiary participation and their contribution. Transparency is vital feature of good governance. It requires the system as procedure of making people aware about their rights and details of panchayat functioning. It could be through compulsory display of accounts, details of panchayat activities, proceedings of panchayat and gram sabha meetings, and so on and also through providing certified copies of documents to people. Support system in terms of manpower, infrastructure and logistics is vital for having planning and implementation system at panchayat levels, viz., district, block and gram panchayat. Under manpower support placement of officers and staff of line department with Panchayati Raj Institutions and control over them is important. Infrastructural support will include building for office and conducting meetings, and logistics will include equipments for execution of works in the village and accessories for carrying out various works. Mechanism for resolving conflicts, settling disputes and arbitration is important for two reasons. First to have a forum for settling conflict for harmonious functioning and second, to instill confidence in people that there is an important body to arbitrate about the conflicting or wrong decisions, and that can give direction for rectification. Performance of the local bodies need to be assessed in order to know the direction of process of decentralization and to have clear idea whether the objectives of decentralization are achieved. The indicators of performance have been broadly classified into, capacity of Panchayati Raj members, political environment, planning system, effectiveness of Panchayati Raj Institutions and implementation quality, responsiveness of Panchayati Raj members, attitudinal issues and transparency and accountability system.

Financial Decentralization

Financial decentralization involves devolving powers with regard to taxation, funds and expenditure upon local bodies in order to first improve the financial position then giving them the financial autonomy for planning and implementation as per local needs. Power of taxation is important for augmenting the internal resources of panchayats. The own income of the panchayat broadly includes tax and non–tax revenue. The tax revenue includes property tax, profession tax etc., and non–tax revenue includes water taxes, user charges etc. Sharing of taxes is for those items that are normally collected by the state government and allocation to panchayats. Devolution of funds upon panchayats by the state is important in order to augment financial capacity of panchayats. Financial autonomy is important in order to provide panchayats scope to prepare plans as per local needs and then to make expenditure.

Geographical Decentralization

In geographical decentralization the powers and functions of headquarters are decentralized to the field officers for effective performance. For e.g. most of the powers of the heads of departments of the state government are decentralized to their field officers at the regional and district levels. This facilitates quick decision making keeping in view the local requirements.

Merits of Decentralization

1. A decentralized organization is more responsive to the needs and demands of the local area and the people. It can understand and assess the real problems and can take decisions for their effective solutions.
2. Delegation of authority is an essential aspect of a decentralized organization. The higher level authorities are shared with the lower level organization. The top levels deal with very important matters, whereas the lower levels are left free to tackle less important issues.
3. A decentralized organization encourages innovations as it welcomes ideas and new techniques recommended by the lower levels of the organization. It leads to more interaction among the personnel.

Louis A. Allen observes that a decentralized organization helps to :

(a) Ease the burden on top executives

(b) Facilitate diversification.

(c) Make decisions for effective and fruitful delivery of goods and services.

(d) Encourage development of meaningful talents.

(e) Improvement motivation of people within the organization.

Forms of Decentralization

Many changes occur within political systems.

The first type of change is sometimes called "Decentralization by default". This happens when government institutions become so ineffective, that they fail almost entirely to make the influence of central authorities penetrate down to lower level arenas and people at the grass root level become heartily cynical about government. When this occurs in countries with lively civil societies, voluntary associations or non–governmental organizations (NGOs) at lower levels sometimes step into generate development projects.

The second thing is privatization – the handover of tasks formerly performed by state agencies to the private sector. Therefore, privatization often involves a shift of power and resources from one major centralized power centre to another.

One further type of decentralization, namely delegation of some responsibilities for development programmes or projects to para-statal agencies.

Fourthly, de–concentration refers to the dispersal of agents of higher levels or government into lower level arenas. Parker refers to it as "administrative decentralization".

Next, the term decentralization sometimes refers to downward fiscal transfers, by which higher levels in the system cede influence over budgets and financial decisions to lower levels.

Finally, there is devolution – the transfer of resources and power (and often taxes) to lower level authorities which are largely or wholly independent of higher levels of government, and which are democratic in nature in some way and to some degree.

Decentralization can entail transfer of powers to different levels within political systems. It can be bestowed on one or more intermediate levels (regions and/or sub–regions). When this involves the creation of fully blown governments at the regional levels, it qualifies as federalism. But more limited powers may go to intermediate levels or local levels.

Advantages of Decentralization

1. Bridging the distance between Central and local levels.
2. Decentralization of responsibilities to lower levels facilitating implementation of technical programmes.
3. Enhancing the influence of decentralized bodies in national politics.
4. Ensuring poor, remote regions of fairer representation in national politics.
5. Facilitating local authorities' access to administrative resources at the regional level.
6. Enhancing coordination of development administration from different line ministries.
7. Facilitating complex development projects.
8. Facilitating scaling up from the local level.
9. Facilitating the upward flow of information from the local level and the responsiveness of Central Government.
10. Combating absenteeism and irresponsible behavior by government employees.

11. Enhancing the accountability and responsiveness of regional level bureaucrats.
12. Facilitating poverty alleviation and fairness of minorities.
13. Facilitating fairness to women.
14. Easing the problem of the fore–shortened time perspective of local level politicians.
15. Facilitating collaboration between NGOs and decentralized authorities.
16. Integrating the efforts of local level voluntary associations.
17. Overcoming authoritarian enclaves.
18. Facilitating the integration of local level politicians into national politics.
19. Facilitating the integration of competitive political parties into decentralized institutions.
20. Combating urban bias.

Decentralized Planning and Panchayati Raj Relation

Although the idea of decentralized planning is as old as Gandhian economic thought, attempts at figuring out what it is and how it should be brought about may be said to be recent. Both during the constitution–making process and thereafter since the inception of the planning process in the country, certain hard choices had to be made between the needs of national security, national unity and economic growth, on the one hand and considerations for achieving a measure of re–distribution with growth on the other, so as to bring about the widest distribution of the benefits of development among the masses and with a view to making an impact on the people below the poverty line. In the initial years, this choice has had to be made in favour of requirements of growth. This "top–down approach" in which the planning and decision making functions remained centralized and vertical around the two political levels, namely the Union and the States. Urban local bodies like the municipalities of rural institutions such as the village panchayats are not only a state subject but have also, by and large, functioned as agencies of civic functioning and not as instruments of micro–level planning and development. Thus, this design of the political and developmental set up in the country had left a near vacuum so far as planning at the sub–state level was concerned.

The thinking about decentralized planning was however, not lacking. The Second Five Year Plan discussed in great detail, the concept of a local horizon plan. The Third Five Year Plan explained a methodology of preparing state plan for rural development on the basis of the District and Block Plans. Attempts were made to develop the three–tier panchayati raj system based on the Balwant Rai Mehta Committee recommendations and with it the idea of 'planning from below' gained some currency. But these ideas did not pick up nor were these operationalized as the Panchayati Raj Institutions except in some states, stagnated and declined after the initial enthusiasm in their growth. The inadequacy of planning capabilities was recognized as a major weak link in the chain and the fourth plan outlined the need for strengthening the planning machinery at different levels. A scheme for strengthening the planning machinery at the state level was launched by the Planning Commission in 1972. The Planning Commission also issued guidelines for district planning in 1969.

Since the Fifth Five Year Plan, a number of special area programmes came to be undertaken with some specialized agencies for their implementation. With the emphasis on anti-poverty programmes for the rural areas with their thrust on the provision of basic minimum needs, employment opportunities and the household–oriented beneficiary programmes, the need for decentralized planning efforts came to be increasingly recognized. The removal of un–employment and significant under employment together with an appreciable rise in the standard of living of the masses within a period of 10 years was stated as a major objective of the draft plan 1978–1983. At this stage block level planning was conceived to complement the rural development effort through fuller utilization of local resources for full employment on the one hand and a quick attention to the local problems, on the other. In November 1977, the Planning Commission appointed a working group under the Chairmanship of Prof. M.L. Dantwala to draw up guidelines for Block level planning. Another committee on Panchayati Raj headed by Sri Ashok Mehta was appointed in December 1977. Both the committees submitted the reports to the government around July–August 1978. In implementation, block level planning itself to the IRD programmes, tended to become an 'isolated exercise' without developing adequate links with higher levels of planning.

Decentralization is the inherent idea in democracy. It is democratic decentralization which aims at associating people with the government to the maximum possible extent. In a democratically decentralized system, people have got the right to initiate their own project for local well being and they have the power to execute and operate them in an autonomous manner.

Democratic decentralization is a centrifugal movement. Power moves from the central to the regional and local areas. It aims to entrust local organs created in local areas with powers, local in character. Thus, there is devolution of autonomy from the higher levels of the government to the lower levels.

The authority thus decentralized should be managed by the people directly or indirectly through their representatives. The institutional machinery of democratic decentralization is necessarily elective.

Democratic decentralization takes the form of autonomy to the people at lower levels of structure to take political decisions, to formulate ways to execute it, to manage and control the finances required for it and ultimately to guide and control its administration.

Democratic decentralization is thus a political idea and local self–government is its institutional form. In India, it is the Panchayati Raj Institutions which are the institutional form of democratic decentralization.

Decentralization should be seen as a means of mobilizing people for development work, giving them opportunities and encouraging them in the decision–making for local area development and also facilitating the implementation of national development policies. Importance of the decentralization, particularly in a democratic system of governance, need not to be overemphasized. Local development units can be effective links between the central government and local communities. Greater participation in development planning and management may not only promote national integration by giving people in different regions of a country a greater ability to participate in planning and decision making, but also increase their share in managing the local needs and meeting their aspirations.

3

An Analysis of Process of Decentralization

The 73rd Constitution Amendment Act has heralded a new chapter in the process of decentralization. The Act has provided a broad framework to states within which the Panchayati Raj (PR) institutions at three levels viz., district, block and gram panchayat, can become the units of development planning and implementation. The Act places the onus of its implementation on the states. It is up to a state how it attends to various provisions of the Act, creates the desired capacities of the local institutions to take up the development activities of their respective areas and provides opportunities to people in their villages development. The states have initiated various measures in order to operationalise the Amendment Act. Some of them include the conduct of elections, reservations for the weaker sections, constitution of SEC, SFC and DPC, transfer of functions and powers, and so on. The implementation of the Act varies in terms of content from state to state. However, there is definite trend towards decentralizing the development system in the rural areas.

In chapters three and four, all the dimensions of decentralization – political, functional, administrative and financial – have been covered. This chapter attempts to critically analyse the following issues in each of the dimensions :

- **Political Decentralization**
  - ➢ Election to local bodies
  - ➢ Status of PR members
  - ➢ People's participation

- ➢ Tenure of chairpersons of panchayats
- ➢ Representation to weaker sections'
- ➢ Size of the gram panchayats
- ➢ MLAs and MPs as members of panchayat bodies
- ➢ Elections to the members to intermediate and district panchayats
- ➢ Accountability of PR members

- **Functional Decentralization**
  - ➢ Transfer of functions
  - ➢ Inter-tier demarcation of functions
  - ➢ Assigning subject-specific responsibilities
- **Administrative Decentralization**
  - ➢ Institutional mechanism for planning
  - ➢ Mechanism for implementation, coordination and monitoring
  - ➢ Manpower support and capabilities of functionaries
  - ➢ Delivery system at the gram panchayat level
  - ➢ Transparency system
  - ➢ Institutional mechanism for resolving conflicts, settling disputes and arbitration
- **Financial Decentralization**
  - ➢ Collection of taxes
  - ➢ Devolution of funds
  - ➢ SFC
  - ➢ Financial autonomy

The detailed description about the above dimensions is given below:

Analysis of Political Decentralization

Election to Local Bodies: The elections to panchayats have been held in most of the states, while in Assam and Bihar the elections were held after gaps of 9 and 23 years respectively. In Andhra Pradesh and Madhya Pradesh, the elections were delayed due to petitions in the court. In Karnataka, these were delayed due to reorganization of gram panchayats. In the state of Gujarat, the elections were not held simultaneously for all the three tiers, and the elections for gram panchayats were held in December, 2001, while the elections for intermediate and zilla panchayats were held in 2000. Similarly, in Punjab, the elections for intermediate and zilla panchayats were delayed due to petition in the courts.

The above are pointers to the fact that neither the elections are held in time nor held simultaneously for all the three tiers. It clearly indicates that the constitutional provisions of timely elections (Article 243 E) and the bar to court intervention (Article 243 O) have not been followed in the right spirit. And such a state will clearly undermine the continuity of the panchayats.

It has also come out during the field study that the election process is mainly sending representatives from the elite class or from political groups. Besides, the weaker sections, though their members get elected, find it hard to have their voice in the panchayats and get marginalized, and their participation remains mainly in the reserved seats and basically during election time. Similarly, the common person finds it hard to get the opportunity to contest election in a highly sensitive and surcharged political environment. The voices of common person who are concerned for village development do not get much attention during the election process. What is equally distressing is the means employed to win the elections, which among others include money, liquor and muscle power.

Status of PR Members: In all the states, in conformity with the 73rd Constitution Amendment Act, the State Acts have provided executive position to PR members.

People's Participation: It is evident from the field studies that the functioning of gram sabha, a fulcrum of participatory development, is far from satisfactory, rather it is something that needs immediate attention. The poor attendance, lack of visible people's participation and the discussion on narrow agenda in the gram sabha present a poor account of functioning of panchayats at the grassroots level. The PR members are more concerned with the devolution of funds and functions, and control over officers and staff for the transfer and postings, rather than the involvement of people at every stage of development.

Moreover, as regards the discussion in the gram sabha, the proceedings are dominated by the discussion on the selection of beneficiaries or construction works. While other vital issues such as: how the education among poor can be improved; how the health and sanitation in the village can be improved; how the crop yield can be enhanced; how the income of landless people can be increased, and so on, do not find much importance in the discussion during the gram sabha. And very little importance is given to look into the issues that are vital for the village development. But people cannot be blamed as adequate efforts have not been made to train the PR members or make people aware about the development needs in a holistic manner.

The functioning of gram sabha can be summed up as a forum where not many people attend or even like to attend the gram sabha meeting, even if they attend they find it hard to participate in the discussion, also the discussion is confined to a few issues and many vital issues of village development are overlooked.

Of particular importance is the issue of structure of gram sabha. It is a forum for eliciting the people's problems and needs, for having transparent way of informing people about the activities of gram panchayat and making PR representatives accountable to the people in the open forum. But, as indicated by field studies, it has its own limitations like: *first*, sheer large number of members makes it difficult (if the large number, say 200-300, of people attend the meetings) to organize meetings smoothly; *second*, these is difficulty in eliciting the views of people, especially of women and other weaker sections, due to dominance by vocal and influential people, and *third*, the planning which is a specialized exercise cannot be handled in gram sabha meeting along. Quite often, the discussion leads to chaotic turn and goes beyond the control of the chairpersons of gram panchayats.

The above description is a clear reflection of less importance given to people's participation in the operational terms.

Tenure of Chairpersons of Panchayats: In certain states one feature has been noticed that the duration of chairpersons of panchayats has been fixed by state government for a certain period. For instance, in Karnataka, it is fixed for twenty months for chairpersons of taluk (intermediate) and zilla panchayats, and thirty months for chairpersons of gram panchayats. Similarly, in Maharashtra, for intermediate and zilla panchayats, earlier (in 1999-2000) the term was fixed for one year for intermediate and zilla panchayats, which has been raised to two and a half years. By any account, these are retrograde steps. Now, in this process, chairpersons hardly find sufficient time to perform and members are more occupied in identifying suitable substitutes (for future) than in working for development.

Representation to Weaker Sections: Article 243D makes provision for the reservation of women and SCs and STs and such reservation should be rotated. The states have construed that the rotation can be for every five years. Now, from the practical point of view, it has been noticed that the members from these categories take longer time to learn the official work due to their initial inhibitions and low educational level. Besides, one term is not sufficient for carrying out sufficient development activities if long term view is taken. It discourages members from taking innovative projects as they feels that they have no chance to become members again.

Size of the Gram Panchayat: The issue of size of gram panchayats was felt when it came to making panchayats capable of delivering services to people. Articles 243B and 243C deal with the formation of gram panchayats. It is on the concerned states to decide about the size of the gram panchayat. The states have formed the gram panchayats based on the population criterion. If we look into the average size of the population of one gram panchayat, it is normally in the vicinity of 3000 in most of the states, and only a few states like Assam, Kerala and West Bengal have population more than 10,000.

Now, if we examine critically, the small size of gram panchayats causes some practical problems for the gram panchayats to function effectively. *First,* the panchayats have not got the relevant staff for providing basic services for health, veterinary, drinking water, irrigation, etc., as the departments do not have sufficient number of field functionaries. It is estimated that if all panchayats were to be provided with the staff for these services, the number of field functionaries has to be increased by 4-5 times that would involve large expenditure on salary. *Second,* similarly, there is an acute shortage of infrastructure for the basic services to be provided to people, and if it were to be created at the GP level, it would require huge investment. *Third,* with so many panchayats, it becomes difficult to organize block level meetings (in which 50 to 100 members participate) and to monitor the financial performance of gram panchayats. Thus, from the points of view of financial, administrative and functional viability, it is vital that necessary support system should be provided to all the gram panchayats. And presently the size of gram panchayat is such which is making it difficult to make them viable units of development.

***MLAs* and *MPs as Members of Panchayat Bodies*:** As per Article 243C, the states have made provision for the representation of MPs and MLAs in the panchayats at intermediate and district levels. In this regard, during field visits several objections have been raised by the panchayat members, as they feel overwhelmed and marginalized by the presence of MLAs and MPs in the panchayat meetings.

Election of Members of Intermediate and Zilla Panchayat: The field studies reveal that the election of the intermediate and zilla panchayats have been a subject of discussion among members of gram panchayats. The Article 243C provides for direct election for members at all the three tiers. It stipulates for territorial constituencies for these tiers (while in the states having population less than twenty lakhs, the intermediate panchayats may be done away). Thus, the intermediate and district panchayats have electoral constituencies that are formed after combining the group of panchayats. Based on the field study, if we examine the present system of multi-level constituencies and the functioning of panchayats at all the three tiers, the following points emerge:

- *First,* the electoral constituencies of intermediate and zilla panchayats are simply geographical boundaries without any logical basis.
- *Second,* mere election of more members to higher tiers cannot be the criterion for more people's participation. While, by any logic the gram panchayats, which are the basic units of development, should get full representation in all the three tiers.
- *Third,* although the chairpersons of gram panchayats have been made the members of the intermediate panchayats and similarly the chairpersons of intermediate panchayats have been made the members of the district panchayat, still it is not effective due to the following reasons:
    - ➢ In states where the chairpersons of the lower panchayats are mere members without any voting right, then the concerned gram panchayats are not given true representation in the higher tiers for all practical purposes.
    - ➢ Even if the chairpersons of the lower panchayats have voting rights, they are not effective in the decision-making as the elected members of the higher panchayats have their own priority.

Besides, the agenda for discussion is decided by the higher panchayat, which may not necessarily address the problems of lower tiers.

- ➢ The number (which varies from 50 to 100 of members) in the higher tiers has become so large that it makes it difficult to conduct the panchayat meetings at intermediate and zilla panchayat levels meaningfully.
- ➢ The views of the chairpersons of gram panchayats are not duly attended to by the higher tiers. While, in the gram sabha, which is the forum of accountability, it is the chairperson of the gram panchayat who has to answer to the questions of people. Thus, in a way the members who have to answer in the gram sabha do not have much say in the proceedings of higher tiers. In a way, it is irrational.

- *Fourth*, what is equally inconsistent is that the elected members of the higher tiers need not be from the same constituency in some states where they are contesting (and may contest from anywhere in the panchayat area in some states e.g., in the state of Karnataka) but they should be in the electoral list of the intermediate or zilla panchayat as the case may be. In this process the members for the intermediate and zilla panchayats mainly contest more from the consideration of caste or religion or political influence, and the desired consideration of people's needs and aspirations or their participation takes backseat.

Accountability of PR Members: For observing financial accountability, Article 243J provides that the state may make provisions for the maintenance of accounts by panchayats and the auditing of such accounts. Accordingly, the audit section of the concerned panchayati raj department carries out the financial audit. The audit involves inspection of books of accounts, checking of vouchers, the procedure of purchases made, etc. This procedure of audit is very much resented by the chairpersons of panchayats as they find themselves in a difficult position to give account for each item, and sometimes they are harassed by the auditors.

In some states, the provisions for the social audit have been made but except in Kerala it has not taken proper shape. It is observed that so far there is no well-established system of making the chairpersons and the members of the gram panchayat accountable to people. Also, the decisions of members of higher tiers (intermediate and zilla panchayats) are not subjected to the scrutiny by the people in the gram sabha, while those decisions might affect the gram panchayats.

Analysis of Functional Decentralization

The full transfer of functions under twenty-nine subjects has not taken place in almost all the states. Even, in the functional terms, the subjects under basic needs (like primary education, health, agriculture veterinary, irrigation, etc.) have not been transferred. Also, inter-tier demarcation of functions has not been carried out resulting into overlapping of functions and conflicts in certain cases. Similarly, subject-specific responsibilities have not been assigned to each tier. In the absence of these vital aspects the panchayats are not in a position to take up the responsibilities under various subjects.

Regarding the issues of subjects under Eleventh Schedule, there are twenty-nine subjects that need to be transferred to panchayats. A careful examination indicates that this Schedule is asking for big responsibilities from the panchayats which range from education, to health, to natural resources management, to handloom and handicraft, to small scale industries, to rural electrification. If we look at the capacity of panchayats, it is too large a responsibility to deliver and needs to be reviewed.

Analysis of Administrative Decentralization

The issues studied under administrative decentralization point towards how inadequate are measures that are initiated by the state governments to provide administrative authority to panchayats. Some of the critical observation have been summed up as follows:

Institutional Mechanism for Planning

Under this the issues of planning process, role of gram sabha, support system and district planning committee have been examined.

- The purpose of the participatory planning at the gram panchayat level is to bring out the critical issues of the importance to community with the involvement of people, so the prepared plan represents the felt-needs and aspirations of all the groups of the village and also the plan so prepared would be sustainable for the socio-economic development of the people. While, as revealed by the field studies, the concept of development planning at the panchayat level or at higher tiers seems to be completely missing. The studies have brought out the deficiencies in the present system of planning at local levels, the prominent among them include: *First,* there is no laid down process of planning for the action plan preparation at all the three tiers, and the planning exercise begins by inviting proposals from the departments without having any emphasis on analysis of data, inter-sectoral needs, etc. And the planning methodology for reaching the rational allocation of funds is not formulated. *Second,* the database that is the basic requirement for the planning is not developed for undertaking planning exercise. *Third,* the infrastructure is in terms of adequate office building, record room for data-storage and facilities such as computers for data analysis and networking, is missing at the block and gram panchayat levels, and only partially some facilities are available at the district level, which are also not enough to carry out any meaningful planning exercise. And *finally,* the planning which is a specialized exercise involving good knowledge and skills is not supported by adequate and trained manpower. Besides, participatory part of planning at gram panchayat is hampered by a number of factors such as: lack of awareness among people, poor people's participation, lack of capabilities in elected members and influence (over decision-making) of some individuals in the gram sabha meeting.

- Integration of plans of three tiers which is very important in order to provide organic linkages to the plans of three tiers and also to assess the overall requirement of funds for the districts is not carried out. No efforts are made for the preparation of database; and the sectoral, backward and forward linkages, and inter-sectoral analyses are not attempted. The district plan is merely a compilation of proposals received from various departments, blocks and the gram panchayats.
- At the grassroots level, another dimension of lack of convergence of resources and services has been added due to the problems of multiple schemes, multiplicity of departments, and resource-gap and missing links within the programmes. The lack of convergence leads to inefficient utilization of resources and lack of availability of services to people. The development efforts continue without addressing this crucial issue of convergence that has strong bearing on the effectiveness and the efficiency of implementation of development programmes. It is a great challenge as to how the village development planning should be carried out in order to ensure not only the optimal allocation of resources but also the convergence of resource for their efficient end-use.
- ***District Planning Committee***: For setting up of District Planning Committee (DPC), some steps have been taken by the states, but there are certain shortcomings in its formation. *First,* though the DPC has to look into

the preparation of district plan based on the local needs, yet the chairperson of DPC is not an elected member from panchayats or municipalities in most of the states. *Second,* in spite of the fact that the planning requires specialized knowledge and skills, DPC does not have adequate experts as its members in order to provide technical inputs and make analyses for reaching rational decision-making. *Third,* DPC is formed but the supporting wing in the form of planning unit is not adequately placed. And, *finally,* no planning committee or unit exists at the block or GP level in order to carry out local level planning and also to provide vital inputs on local needs and resources to DPC.

Mechanism for Implementation, Coordination and Monitoring: For the implementation of programmes issues like beneficiaries' participations in the execution of work and procedure of supervision have not been addressed. The implementation of programmes is carried out by the gram panchayats through chairpersons or departments and in some cases the contractors also execute the works disregarding the involvement of beneficiaries. While the people's participation is very important, the beneficiaries' involvement at the execution and supervision stages remains negligible in all the states, with the exception of Kerala. Also, due to lack of administrative management, coordination between PRIs and the line departments remains a problem in the planning and implementation of programmes. Similarly, the monitoring system, in order to assess the progress of works, is not rightly placed causing problems in knowing the physical and financial status of the projects/works.

Manpower Support and Capabilities of Functionaries

- To begin with, the placement of officers and staff of line department with PRIs has not yet been done except in a few cases in some states. In the absence of control of panchayats over the field staff of line departments, the panchayats find it difficult to implement and supervise various programmes. Besides, if we examine the available manpower at the block and gram panchayat levels, there is no addition to the strength of field staff since 1950s i.e. the time of community development programme, while there has been manifold increase in the officers and staff at the State and at the Central levels. In other words, at the cutting edge level, where the implementation of programmes takes place there is no improvement in the strength of manpower.

Table 3.1. Problem Areas in Development Planning and Implementation at Panchayat Level

Sl.	*Areas*	*Items*	*Problems*
1.	Functioning of Gram Sabha	(i) Participation	: People hardly participate in gram sabha as they are disorganized and unaware
		(ii) Role of women	: Women do not attend meetings. Only a few people dominate the proceedings.
2.	Planning	(i) Data Collection	: Proper data schedules not available and lack of facility in storage of data
		(ii) Data Analysis	: Tools and techniques are not known at local level
		(iii) Problem identification	: Only listing the problems without sequencing
		(iv) Prioritization	: No objective criteria is applied
		(v) Project formulation	: Not able to do in the absence of proper knowledge
		(vi) Plan preparation	: No inter-sectoral and backward and forward linkages analyses are carried out
		(vii) Resource mobilization	: Not able to do through public contribution and other agencies

3.	Implementation	(i)	Plan scheduling	: Not prepared
		(ii)	Beneficiaries committee	: Not properly formed
		(iii)	Training to executing of beneficiaries committee	: Training is not given
		(iv)	Manpower and logistics support	: Work is started without looking into the details
4.	Monitoring	(i)	Monitoring team	: No earmarked team
		(ii)	Monitoring formats	: No user-friendly formatting is done
		(iii)	Data analysis	: Proper data analysis is not done.
5.	Evaluation	(i)	Evaluation team	: No earmarked team
		(ii)	Evaluation of data analysis	: Data analysis is not done to reach logical conclusion. No action for improvement in scheme-design is taken.
6.	MIS	(i)	Identification of critical information	: No data feeding, analysis and reporting system exists, to reach quick decision-making
		(ii)	Flow of Information	

- ***Administrative Control over Field Officers and Staff***: In some states (e.g. Madhya Pradesh, Maharashtra) the district-level officers have been designated as Addl. CEOs, zilla parishad, and they are required to report to ZP. Also, Zilla Parishad has been given powers of transfer and postings of district and lower level functionaries. Besides, the field level functionaries have been asked to report to the concerned tier where their office is situated. In this context, the two important observations have emerged. These are:
  (i) The district-level officers find it difficult to control their lower level functionaries due to multiplicity of control. As the works of field functionaries are now supervised and monitored by various institutions like GP, Block, ZP and

their own departments. Under such state, sometimes, simultaneously all give instructions, which may not necessarily be in harmony with each other, to field staff and officers. Such situations, in many cases, have resulted into confusion in performing duty at the GP level.

(ii) The panchayat functionaries report to the gram panchayat where they are posted while they are supposed to work for 3-5 GPs (as normally one field functionary of a particular department is in-charge of more than one GP). Thus, while working in all the panchayats of their jurisdictions, the functionaries are not accountable to those gram panchayats where they are not reporting.

- ***Syndrome of achieving Somehow Target, and Touch and Go***: In the present setup of development the field officers and staff are not having proper direction for development. Their work basically pertains to, first, identifications of beneficiaries, then giving work-order, and finally, doing check-measurements. This is all very mechanical and there is a 'touch and go' tendency in them, and the focus of the work remains on achieving target somehow. Moreover, there is no concern among functionaries for issues like people's participation, quality of work, whether the beneficiaries are getting the intended benefits, etc. They practically have no knowledge of how the people are to be involved in the development process — village level planning, project formulation, management of implementation, monitoring and evaluation. Work just, goes on on an *ad hoc* basic, without any planning with the sole objective of achieving the physical target. What is equally distressing is that the field officers are not trained to handle the task of village panchayat and the sole criterion of judging the performance is target achieved by the field officers and staff.

In addition, the much-needed subject-specific specialized knowledge in planning and management of programmes is very badly missing in the field functionaries. It is precisely one of the crucial factors, why the implementation of programmes suffers. As a result, programme objectives are not fully achieved.

Transparency: Though all the states have provided provisions for transparency, yet these have not been translated into action. For example, in case of gram sabha, in some states some of the decisions that are taken in the open meeting are not reflected in the proceedings, in some other cases the proceedings are not made available to people, the necessary physical and financial details are not displayed outside the panchayat office, and so on.

Delivery System at the Gram Panchayat Level: At the gram panchayat level, delivery system is poor as far as the availability of services for health, education, agriculture veterinary, drinking water, irrigation, bank loan, PDS, etc. is concerned. People have to struggle very hard for these basic services. The reasons, as analyzed from the study include: *first*, poor infrastructure at the GP level; *second*, inadequate manpower (e.g. the teachers or health workers or agricultural workers are not posted in the required number); *third*, lack of logistics support; *fourth*, lack of proper administrative system (delegation of responsibilities and transfer of power, etc.); and *finally*, poor people's participation. Here, it needs to be recognized that mere placement of funds will yield result is not possible in the absence of proper delivery mechanism at the village level. And, more specifically, how presently the PR institutions are handicapped in ensuring the delivery of services to people is illustrated (Gupta, 2003). The following examples would further substantiate how the services are affected due to poor service mechanism:

Agriculture programme is handicapped by a number of constraints. *Firstly*, by non-availability of inputs viz., seeds, fertilizer, pesticide and credit at one point. *Secondly*, by necessity of availing technical guidance from multiple departments viz., agriculture, horticulture, soil conservation, irrigation and agro-industries. And, *thirdly*, by dependence on multiple programmes such as watershed development, seed multiplication programme, special area programme, special crop development programmes and so on. With this kind of an approach, the beneficiaries have to run to a number of places for availing technical services and inputs. And, moreover, many of them do no get the desired benefits.

Health services are denied to people due to a number of reasons such as lack of health centre, non-placement of doctors or health workers and non-availability of medicines or equipments. In several cases it is found that some or the other item is missing and all the items are not placed at one place in order to provide a full package that would deliver health services to people with ease. It is often noticed that people prefer to go to a private doctor than to go to a public health centre.

Children are deprived of primary education due to scarcity of adequate buildings, want of teaching-aids and poor environment around the school. New buildings are added (moreover, in many cases the quality of construction is poor) without providing full facilities to schools in order to make them fully functional. For instance, due to paucity of funds and a desire to cover large number of villages, schools are provided with 2-3 rooms, and similarly because of shortage of teachers, normally 2-3 teachers are posted. Together with this, teaching-aids are not adequately provided, leave alone proper environment and sports facilities. Now, under such circumstances the schools are rendered ineffective and leave teachers discouraged, parents unenthusiastic and children disinterested. There is only quantitative addition but no qualitative improvement. Similarly, veterinary services are not made available to people due to poor infrastructural, equipments and medicinal support. And, due to want of logistics support, the field staff find it hard to organize field-camps.

Table 3.2. Causal-Matrix Indicating the Availability of Services to People

S.No.	*Causes*	*Type of Services Affected*
1.	If buildings are created, either they are not having sufficient space or lack electricity or water facilities, or officers and staff are not posted in desired number.	Health centres, Primary schools, Veterinary services
2.	Even if officers and staff are posted, they might be either not having sufficient training to carry out the desired job or lacking the requisite supporting infrastructure or equipments for enabling them to provide services to people.	Watershed development, Development planning Primary education
3.	It is found in some cases that infrastructural or manpower support system is available but is located either at inconvenient locations or in a scattered manner, that deprives people from availing the services.	Banks, Agricultural inputs
4.	In certain other cases, programme requires the support of various departments and each of them may not extend the same due to either lack of funds or non-availability of support system, or lack of coordination.	Watershed development, Infrastructural development, IRDP (now SGSY)
5.	In some specific cases of education and extension, there is often lack of logistic support and extension-aids that restrict the reach of field functionaries to the intended target.	IEC, Training
6.	Due to inefficient management of implementation, the services may not reach in time or in the desired sequence.	Immunization, Childcare and nutritional programme (ICDS)

Analysis of Financial Decentralization

Analysis of Panchayat Taxes

Tax-base and Per Capita Income: The per capita tax collection for all the three tiers together is significantly high in the states of Haryana, Kerala and Punjab and the figures are Rs. 32.92, Rs. 34.16 and Rs. 25.64 respectively. The same figure (which is less than Rs. 5.0), is very low in the states of Assam, Madhya Pradesh, Orissa, Uttar Pradesh and West Bengal. In other states, the collection is not that good but in Andhra Pradesh and Maharashtra, it is quite encouraging.

When we look at the tax collection at the gram panchayat level, the tax-base is higher in the states of Haryana, Kerala and Punjab. The per capita tax collection is about Rs. 32.88 for Haryana, Rs. 34.16 for Kerala and Rs. 21.95 for Punjab. While in the states of Assam, Orissa, Madhya Pradesh, Rajasthan, Uttar Pradesh and West Bengal, the per capita collection is quite low and it varies from Rs. 0.28 to Rs. 4.11. If we look at the intermediate panchayat (IP) level, the average per capita tax collection Rs. 0.45, which is a pittance. As regards the collection of taxes at the district panchayat (DP) level, this figure is very low and is less than Rs. 3.0 in almost all the states. In Kerala, IP and DP have not been assigned responsibilities for tax collection.

Thus, the tax-base for the collection of local taxes is low in most of the states and it is comparatively better in the states of Haryana, Kerala and Punjab. The low tax-base is reflection of low capacity of taxpayers to pay and also that of tax collection authority to collect taxes.

Contribution by Gram Panchayats in the Total Tax Collection: The contribution of tax collection by the gram panchayats in the total tax collection forms the majority with the exception of Uttar Pradesh and Rajasthan, especially the former. The all India average figure is about 84.00 per cent. In Uttar Pradesh, the collection is very less due to lesser demand made by the gram panchayats for local taxes.]

Percentage Annual Increase of Collection of Taxes: At the gram panchayat level the percentage annual increase of collection of taxes is quite high in the states of Andhra Pradesh (15.12), Kerala (27.25), Madhya Pradesh (16.38), Maharashtra (29.05), Punjab (19.16) and Tamil Nadu (18.24). When we look at the tax collection for all the tiers, the same states have higher percentage of annual increase. These percentages are much lower in both the cases in the states of Assam (1.76), Rajasthan (-2.44), Orissa (2.24) and West Bengal (6.25). Overall, the percentage increase is low in majority of the states. In Maharashtra, it has picked up in the recent years due to enhanced rates of property and water taxes (based on field study). What is significant here is that not only the tax-base is low but also rate of increase is low in most of the cases. Besides, both (tax-base and percentage increase) are less in the same states such as Assam, Orissa, Rajasthan, Uttar Pradesh and West Bengal, which is a matter of serious concern.

If we look at the collection of taxes in Haryana and Punjab, it is mainly on account of panchayat own property i.e. agricultural and (which is leased out on rent) while the income from tax revenue is comparatively very low. It reflects low contribution by individuals in the form of taxes, which is not a healthy sign (based on field study).

Own Income as Percentage of Total Income: The total income earned by the panchayats at all the three tiers is miniscule in most of the states except in Assam, Haryana, Kerala and Punjab. The figure (22.32%) in respect of Assam is high, it is basically the reflection of low income from other sources or in other words the grants given to panchayats is less. Though this percentage is lower in case of Kerala vis-à-vis Haryana and Punjab but it is due to significantly high grants which is several time more than that in other two states. The lower percentage in other states is a reflection of high dependence on government grants and their low internal resources.

Table 3.3. Collection of Taxes by All Tiers in Different States

S.N.	Name of the state	Tax Collection (Rs. In lakhs) 1990-91	1994-95	1997-98	Per capita (1997-98) (Rs.)	Average %age annual increase	Status (High/ Medium/ Low)
1.	Andhra Pradesh	6269.57	9294.67	13779.69	20.87	14.98	Medium
2.	Assam	300.96	326.05	345.99	1.54	1.95	Very low
3.	Gujarat	2745.07	3366.38	4036.11	9.77	5.90	Low
4.	Haryana	2939.00	4272.00	5301.00	32.92	10.05	High
5.	Karnataka	1733.05	2464.47	3013.72	6.69	9.12	Low
6.	Kerala	3131.51	5561.33	9909.34	34.16	27.25	High
7.	Madhya Pradesh	1194.17	2581.22	3203.83	4.85	21.50	Very low
8.	Maharashtra	3420.51	6306.88	11217.00	14.19	28.35	Medium
9.	Orissa	590.37	801.90	699.38	2.18	2.24	Very low
10.	Punjab	2155.70	4533.16	5386.62	25.64	18.35	High
11.	Rajasthan	2427.61	2554.04	3074.57	6.98	3.25	Low
12.	Tamil Nadu	1571.59	2471.15	3403.77	6.07	14.15	Low
13.	Uttar Pradesh	2275.35	3902.67	4665.17	3.35	13.05	Very low
14.	West Bengal	1423.42	1457.67	1959.21	2.88	4.68	Very low
	All India	37036.41	47794.06	67707.85	9.02	10.12	Low

Source: Calculation based on data from EFC Report, 2000.

Table 3.4. Collection of Taxes by Gram Panchayats in Different States

S.N.	Name of the state	Tax Collection (Rs. In lakhs) 1990-91	1994-95	1997-98	Per capita (1997-98) (Rs.)	%age of total collection (1997-98)	Average %age annual increase
1.	Andhra Pradesh	5219.81	7694.67	11650.09	17.65	84.55	15.12
2.	Assam	204.48	221.33	234.85	1.04	67.87	1.76
3.	Gujarat	2036.48	2479.84	3158.25	7.64	78.25	6.89
4.	Haryana	2939.00	4272.00	5295.00	32.88	99.88	9.98
5.	Karnataka	1733.05	2464.47	3013.72	6.69	100.00	9.12
6.	Kerala	3131.51	5561.33	9909.34	34.16	100.00	27.25
7.	Madhya Pradesh	1171.70	2343.32	2718.24	4.11	84.86	16.38
8.	Maharashtra	3169.73	5733.14	10550.38	13.35	94.05	29.05
9.	Orissa	590.37	801.90	699.38	2.18	100.00	2.24
10.	Punjab	1815.71	3951.96	4610.30	21.95	85.59	19.16
11.	Rajasthan	1672.00	1305.00	1344.00	3.05	43.72	-2.44
12.	Tamil Nadu	1031.82	1845.01	2575.30	4.59	75.66	18.24
13.	Uttar Pradesh	332.20	484.26	382.13	0.28	8.19	1.89
14.	West Bengal	859.07	853.81	1296.51	1.90	66.14	6.25
	All India	31562.79	39161.55	56880.50	7.58	84.00	10.05

Source: Calculation based on data from EFC Report, 2000.

Table 3.5. Collection of Taxes by Intermediate Panchayats in Different States

S.No.	*Name of the state*	*Tax Collection (Rs. In lakhs)*			*Per capita (1997-98) (Rs.)*
		1990-91	*1994-95*	*1997-98*	
1.	Andhra Pradesh	262.44	400.00	532.40	0.80
2.	Assam	96.48	104.72	111.14	0.49
3.	Gujarat	169.96	254.03	357.81	0.86
4.	Haryana	0.00	0.00	0.00	0.00
5.	Karnataka	0.00	0.00	0.00	0.00
6.	Kerala	0.00	0.00	0.00	0.00
7.	Madhya Pradesh	17.18	224.78	428.81	0.65
8.	Maharashtra	73.87	134.13	188.43	0.23
9.	Orissa	0.00	0.00	0.00	0.00
10.	Punjab	255.10	461.10	550.17	2.61
11.	Rajasthan	631.37	924.40	1230.37	2.72
12.	Tamil Nadu	539.77	626.14	828.47	1.47
13.	Uttar Pradesh	0.00	0.00	0.00	0.00
14.	West Bengal	298.89	328.47	408.49	0.60
	All India	1713.69	2533.37	3405.72	0.45

Source: Calculation based on data from EFC Report, 2000.

Table 3.6. Collection of Taxes by District Panchayats in Different States

S.N.	*Name of the state*	*Tax Collection (Rs. In lakhs)*			*Per capita (1997-98) (Rs.)*
		1990-91	*1994-95*	*1997-98*	
1	*2*	*3*	*4*	*5*	*6*
1.	Andhra Pradesh	787.32	1200.00	1597.20	2.41
2.	Assam	0.00	0.00	0.00	0.00
3.	Gujarat	538.63	632.51	520.05	1.25
4.	Haryana	0.00	0.00	6.00	0.04

1	2	3	4	5	6
5.	Karnataka	0.00	0.00	0.00	0.00
6.	Kerala	0.00	0.00	0.00	0.00
7.	Madhya Pradesh	5.29	13.12	56.78	0.09
8.	Maharashtra	176.90	439.60	478.20	0.61
9.	Orissa	0.00	0.00	0.00	0.00
10.	Punjab	84.89	120.10	226.15	1.07
11.	Rajasthan	124.24	324.64	500.20	1.24
12.	Tamil Nadu	0.00	0.00	0.00	0.00
13.	Uttar Pradesh	1943.15	3418.41	4283.04	3.08
14.	West Bengal	265.46	275.39	254.21	0.37
	All India	3759.93	6099.13	7421.63	0.99

Source: Calculation based on data from EFC Report, 2000.

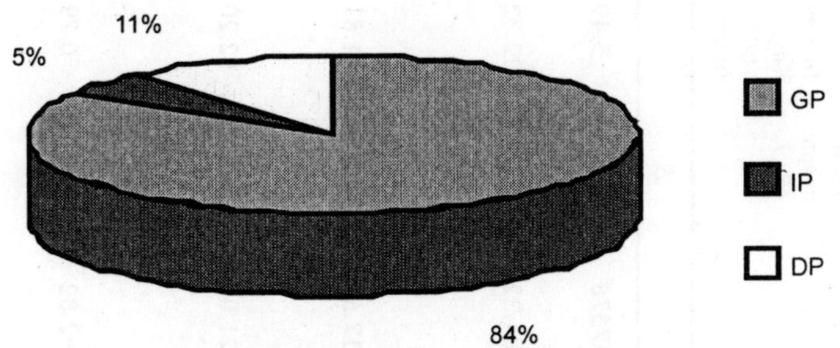

Fig. 3.1. Share of each Tier in the total Own Revenue of Panchayats (1997-98)

Source: Based on data given in EFC Report, 2000.

Contribution of own Tax vis-à-vis own Non-tax Income: It is important to know the composition of tax collection by the panchayats in order to know the tax income from 'personal income or property of business' on one hand, and the tax income from 'panchayat property and services (like health, drinking water, irrigation, panchayat land, etc.) provided by the panchayats', on the other. The former represents the capacity of people to pay for their own income or property, while the latter represents the capacity of the panchayats (local

Table 3.7. Own Income vis-à-vis Total Income in Different States (1997-98)

S.No.	*Name of the state*	*Own income (Rs.)*	*Other income (Rs.)*	*Total income (Rs.)*	*Own Income %age of total income*	*Remarks*	*Overall rating of own income*
1	*2*	*3*	*4*	*5*	*6*	*7*	*8*
1.	Andhra Pradesh	13779.69	237378	251158.57	5.49	Good own income but low contribution in total income.	Good
2.	Assam	345.99	1204.32	1550.31	22.32	Very low own income but higher percentage of total income due to low availability of funds with panchayats.	Poor
3.	Gujarat	4036.11	219217.60	223253.71	1.81	Low own income and low contribution in total income of panchayats.	Poor
4.	Haryana	5301.00	3221.00	8522.00	62.20	High own income and very high contribution in total income of panchayats (but low other income).	Very Good
5.	Karnataka	3013.72	373792.82	376806.54	0.79	Low own income and low contribution in total income of panchayats.	Poor

1	2	3	4	5	6	7	8
6.	Kerala	9909.34	88367.25	98276.59	10.09	High income and good contribution in total income of panchayats (but higher income from other source).	Very Good
7.	Madhya Pradesh	3203.83	174697.64	177901.47	1.81	Very low own income and very low contribution in total income of panchayats.	Very Poor
8.	Maharashtra	11217.00	319530.01	330747.02	3.39	Good own income but low contribution in total income of panchayats.	Good
9.	Orissa	699.38	63302.87	64002.25	1.09	Very low own income and very low contribution in total income of panchayats.	Very Poor
10.	Punjab	5386.62	8154.42	13541.04	39.78	High own income and high contribution in total income of panchayats (but low other income).	Very Good
11.	Rajasthan	3074.57	148946.18	152020.75	2.02	Low own income and very low contribution in total income of panchayats.	Very Poor
12.	Tamil Nadu	3403.77	38812.64	42216.41	8.06	Low own income and low contribution in total income of panchayats.	Poor

1	2	3	4	5	6	7	8
13.	Uttar Pradesh	4665.17	83659.19	88324.36	5.28	Very low own income and low contribution in total income of panchayats.	Very Poor
14.	West Bengal	1959.21	46816.25	48775.46	4.02	Very low own income and low contribution in total income of panchayats.	Very Poor
	All India	67707.85	1867846.53	1935554.38	3.49	Low own income and low contribution in total income of panchayats.	Poor

Source: Calculations based on EFC Report, 2000.

Table 3.8. Own Tax and Own Non-tax in Different States (1997-98)

S.No.	Name of the State	Own Income (Rs.)	Owntax (Rs.)	Own non-tax (Rs.)	Owntax as %age of total income	Per capita own tax (Rs.)*	Per capita own non-tax (Rs.)**
1.	Andhra Pradesh	13779.69	7990.07	5789.62	57.12	12.10	8.77
2.	Assam	345.99	342.86	3.13	99.02	1.53	1.39
3.	Gujarat	4036.11	3093.28	942.83	76.15	7.48	2.28
4.	Haryana	5301.00	450.00	4851.00	8.21	2.79	30.13
5.	Karnataka	3013.72	2592.43	421.29	86.23	5.76	0.93
6.	Kerala	9909.34	8755.35	1153.99	88.36	30.19	3.97
7.	Madhya Pradesh	3203.83	1167.10	2036.73	36.45	1.76	3.08
8.	Maharashtra	11217.00	7459.15	3757.86	66.86	9.44	4.75
9.	Orissa	699.38	462.34	237.04	66.25	1.44	0.74
10.	Punjab	5386.62	69.85	5316.77	1.45	0.33	25.31
11.	Rajasthan	3074.57	N.A.	N.A.	N.A.	N.A.	N.A.
12.	Tamil Nadu	3403.77	3293.80	109.97	96.22	5.88	0.19
13.	Uttar Pradesh	4665.17	865.36	3799.81	18.68	0.62	2.73
14.	West Bengal	1959.21	784.61	1174.60	40.12	1.15	1.72
	All India	9707.85	37691.13	30016.72	55.12	5.02	4.00

Source: Calculation based on EFC Report, 2000.

*Higher own tax will reflected the higher own assets or higher own income of people.

**Higher own non-tax will ref lect higher assets (of panchayats) or investment opportunities for the panchayats or more economic activities in panchayat area.

bodies) to charge for their property or for the services provided to people. The Table 3.8 shows that the percentage contribution of own tax to total income is more than 50 in most of the states. The states like Assam, Karnataka, Kerala and Tamil Nadu have very high, more than 85 per cent, own tax contribution that reflects that the contribution from the individuals in higher. While in two states, Haryana and Punjab, this figure is exceptionally low, which reflects that the panchayats generate income from own property and people contribute less from their own income. Higher non-tax collection reflects that the panchayats have higher investment opportunities from their assets or more economic activities in their areas.

Efficiency of Collection of Tax: Efficiency of collection of tax in terms of : (i) coverage of households (under all taxes including user charges) in the tax-net, (ii) percentage collection of demand and (iii) the higher per capita collection is much higher in Kerala. In Kerala, the percentage of households paying taxes is 79% and the collection as percentage of demand is 72%. Though the tax collection is quite high in Haryana and Punjab, but it is mainly from the panchayat property (agricultural land) while the personal tax collection is far less.

In sum, based on the above analysis, the tax collection by panchayats is not satisfactory in all the states except in Kerala.

Correlation of Own Income with State Domestic Product and Infrastructure

There is a direct correlation of own income with state domestic product and the Table 3.9 shows that its value is + 0.62. It shows that the income of people is going to be vital determinant for the panchayats to charge taxes and also to collect them. SDP covers the income in both rural and urban areas, however, such a correlation can be indicative of the direction of the two variables (per capita SDP and per capita own income of panchayats). Similarly, in most of the states, correlation is found with respect to infrastructural status and collection of taxes, and the table shows that these two are in the same direction in most of the states. Also, it is indicated that the states (like Kerala, Punjab) with higher literacy rate are collecting higher taxes.

All these are pointers to the fact that the development policies, that are leading to higher individual income, infrastructural development and increased HRD, are going to result into higher tax collection.

Classification: Based on the own income of panchayats, as per table, the states can be classified as under:

Higher	:	Haryana, Kerala and Punjab
Medium	:	Andhra Pradesh, Maharashtra
Low	:	Karnataka, Rajasthan and West Bengal
Very Low	:	Assam, Gujarat, Orissa, Madhya Pradesh and Uttar Pradesh

Critical Examination of Tax Collection

Based on field study, if we critically examine the collection of taxes, two factors are very crucial, first, the environment; and the second, income distribution. In spite of lower per capita income in Kerala, the tax collection is higher. It is due to above two factors. First, as the people are educated and aware, as well as the panchayats are well conscious about the responsibility of collection of taxes and taking up development works, the people pay tax. It indicates that the people show not only responsibility but also have faith in the abilities of panchayats to deliver services. Therefore, they make contribution as prescribed by the panchayats. Together with this, there is a good political environment in support of it. Second, the income of people in rural areas (in Kerala) is much higher unlike in other states where the income is confined to urban areas (even if the per capita income is lower in this state, there is a good distribution of income).

The own income in Haryana and Punjab is high. The main contribution is from the income from panchayat land. But we need to appreciate that these two states have considerably

Table 3.9. Own Income of Taxes by all Tiers in Different States vis-à-vis Per Capita State Domestic Product (1997-98)

S.No.	*Name of the state*	*Own income of all tiers (Rs. in lakhs)*	*Per capita own income*	*Status of income (High/ Medium/ Low)*	*Per capita state domestic product*	*Infrastructural status at gram panchayat level in the study area*	*Correlation direction between own income vis-à-vis infrastructural status at gram panchayat level*
1.	Andhra Pradesh	13779.69	20.87	Medium	10590	Poor	Not in the same direction
2.	Assam	345.99	1.54	Very low	7335	Poor	Same direction (Positive)
3.	Gujarat	4036.11	9.77	Low	16251	Poor	Same direction (Positive)
4.	Haryana	5301.00	32.92	High	17626	Good	Same direction (Positive)
5.	Karnataka	3013.72	6.69	Low	11693	Good	Not in the same direction
6.	Kerala	9909.34	34.16	High	11936	Very Good	Same direction (Positive)
7.	Madhya Pradesh	3203.83	4.85	Very low	8114	Poor	Same direction (Positive)
8.	Maharashtra	11217.00	14.19	Medium	18365	Poor	Not in the same direction
9.	Orissa	699.38	2.18	Very low	6767	Poor	Same direction (Positive)
10.	Punjab	5386.62	25.64	High	19500	Good	Same direction (Positive)
11.	Rajasthan	3074.57	6.98	Low	9356	Poor	Same direction (Positive)
12.	Tamil Nadu	3403.77	6.07	Low	12989	Poor	Same direction (Positive)
13.	Uttar Pradesh	4665.17	3.35	Very low	7263	Poor	Same direction (Positive)
14.	West Bengal	1959.21	2.88	Very low	10636	Good	Not in the same direction

Source: Calculations based on EFC Report, 2000.

Note:
1. Correlation coefficient between own income of taxes by all tiers in different states vis-à-vis per capita state domestic product: 0.62.
2. Correlation direction between own income of taxes by all tiers in different states vis-à-vis infrastructural status at gram panchayat level: Same direction in most of the states.

high entrepreneurship in agriculture. Moreover, there is a good scope for the success on account of higher income of people as the surplus can find good market. Besides, the panchayats have good established procedure for the collection of the taxes in Haryana and Punjab, it is mainly on account of panchayat own property i.e. agricultural land (which is leased out), while the income from own tax is comparatively much lower. It reflects low contribution by individuals in the form of taxes, which is not a healthy sign.

For other states, the tax collection is not satisfactory. What is significant here is that in most of the states not only the tax-base is low but also increase in annual rate of collection is low. That apart, both (tax-base and percentage increase) are less in the same states such as Assam, Orissa, Rajasthan and West Bengal, which is a matter of serious concern. Also, the states of Assam, Orissa and Rajasthan have low per capita own income, low infrastructural base and low HRD level.

In sum, the above analysis shows that in three states of Haryana, Kerala and Punjab there is a good own income of panchayats which is much above that of in other states. It substantiates an important point that own income (or tax collection) is going to be higher in those panchayats where there is a good income of people, proper environment for tax collection and existence of appropriate tax collection mechanism.

Critical Issues of Financial Decentralization

Degree of Fiscal Decentralization

It can be measured in terms of :

- *Financial autonomy* – Measured by the ratio of local revenue from own sources to total local expenditure.
- *Revenue decentralization* – Measured by the share of local revenue from own sources in total state government revenue.
- *Expenditure decentralization* – Measured by the contribution of total local expenditure to state government expenditure.

Financial Autonomy

For all the tiers, the financial autonomy is significantly low, due to low own income of panchayats. From Table 3.10 below we see that the all-India value of FAR is only 3.25 per cent for all tiers and 10.60 for GPs . Only two states: Haryana (36.50 per cent) and Punjab (33.89 per cent), and to some extent Kerala (13.78 per cent) have some reasonable value of FAR. In Gujarat, Karnataka, Madhya Pradesh, Maharasthra, Orissa and Rajasthan, FAR is lower than the national average. As a natural corollary to low financial autonomy, revenue dependency of panchayats on states and Centre is high. Higher FAR for GPs in comparison to that of all theirs, reflects that GPs are raising own income in excess of other tiers.

Table 3.10. Important Ratios of Panchayat Finances in different States (1997-98)

S.No.	*Name of the States*	*Financial Autonomy Ratio (FAR) (For all tiers)*	*Financial Autonomy Ratio (FAR) (for GPs)*	*Revenue Decentra-lization Ratio (RDR) (for all tiers)*	*Expenditure Decentra-lization Ratio (EDR) (for all tiers)*
1.	Andhra Pradesh	5.58	40.45	0.75	14.10
2.	Gujarat	1.79	53.45	0.28	14.98
3.	Haryana	36.50	38.78	0.67	1.88
4.	Karnataka	0.82	12.37	0.24	29.32
5.	Kerala	13.78	22.49	1.03	7.43
6.	Madhya Pradesh	1.79	3.84	0.23	12.54
7.	Maharashtra	2.45	19.63	0.39	16.56
8.	Orissa	1.09	4.80	0.11	9.33
9.	Punjab	33.89	37.23	0.59	1.67
10.	Rajasthan	2.00	1.64	0.22	12.11
11.	Tamil Nadu	6.94	10.84	0.20	2.81
12.	Uttar Pradesh	5.14	0.51	0.19	3.42
13.	West Bengal	3.55	4.11	0.13	4.08
	All India	3.25	10.60	0.28	9.16

Source: Calculations based on data given in EFC Report, 2000 and CMIE, 2002.

The funds (own income and devolved funds) over which the panchayats have rights to spend as per their own plans are very less in all the states except in Kerala, where per capita availability with the panchayats is Rs. 310.02 (57.50+252.52), the same varies from Rs. 1.25 to Rs. 67.50 in all other states. Thus, the low availability of funds that too coupled with tied form of grants makes it difficult for the panchayats to exercise their financial rights for the projects of local importance.

Similarly, at the all-India level the revenue decentralization ratio (RDR) and expenditure decentralization ratio (EDR) are 0.28% and 9.16% respectively, including low tax collection and expenditure by panchayats vis-à-vis state. What is significantly worrying is the decline in FAR since 1990-91, indicating erosion of autonomy of panchayats.

Table 3.11. Financial Autonomy Ratio (FAR) at the All India Level for Panchayats of All Tiers

Tier	FAR	Remarks
1990–91	5.28	
1993–94	3.62	Decrease in Financial Autonomy
1997–98	3.25	

Source: Calculations based on data given in EFC Report, 2000 and CMIE, 2002.

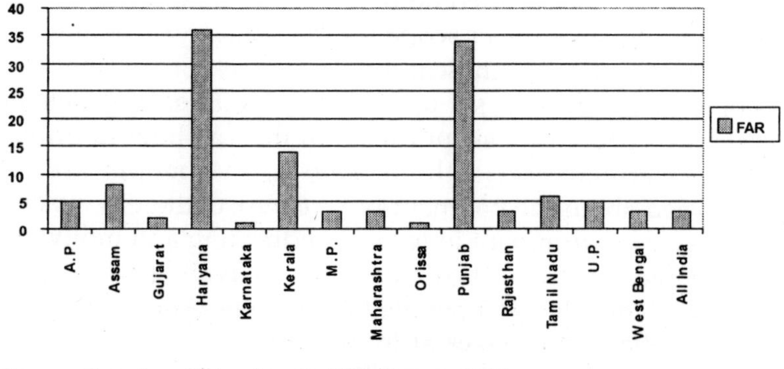

Source : Based on Data given in EFC Report, 2000.

Fig. 3.2. Financial Autonomy Ratio (of All Tiers) (1997–98)

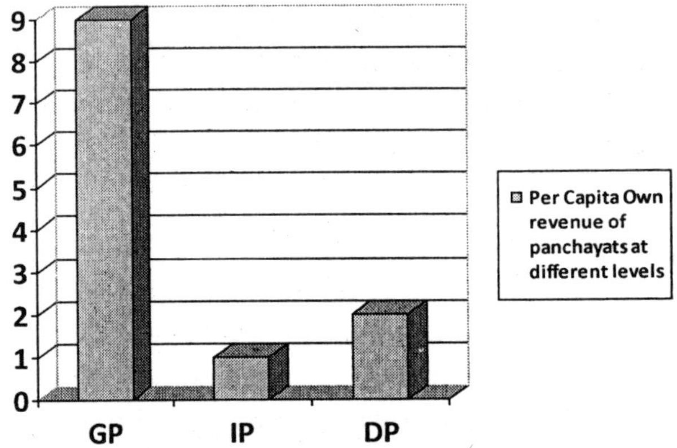

Source: Based on data given in EFC Report, 2000.

Fig. 3.3. Per Capita Own Revenue of Panchayats at Different Tiers (1997–98)

Collection of Taxes: Under Article 243H the state may authorize the panchayats to impose and collect taxes. States have made provisions for the collection of taxes by the panchayats. However, the present status of panchayats finances is marked with low tax-base and poor institutional arrangements. If we examine carefully the poor state of collection of taxes, it will reveal that it is due to combination of various factors such as: *First,* lack of political will as there is a fear of losing popularity in the event of imposing taxes. *Second,* the existing income-base of the panchayats is very low, which leaves lesser scope for the panchayats to augment their income level significantly. *Third,* lack of confidence of people in the present set-up or PR institutions and delivery system, as people are skeptical about their abilities to provide services effectively to them. *Fourth,* the people are less concerned about the payment of taxes. Also, there is a lack of conducive environment in terms of educating and motivating the people for giving taxes in order to avail services. *Fifth,* the low income level of people to pay taxes. And, *finally,* high cost of collection of taxes at local levels.

If we examine the per capita total collection of taxes (tax and non-tax revenue) by all the tiers, it varies from Rs. 1.54

in Assam to Rs. 34.16 in Kerala, while all India average stands at Rs. 9.02. Likewise, the all India average per capita tax collection by gram panchayats, intermediate panchayats and district panchayats is Rs. 7.58, Rs. 0.45 and Rs. 0.99 respectively. It can be seen from the table that the collection of taxes is satisfactory in Kerala and to some extent in Punjab and Haryana. The own income as percentage of total income varies from 0.79 in Karnataka to 62.20 in Haryana. Though the percentage level is high in case of Haryana, but the total income in this state is comparatively much lower (due to low value of devolved funds) in comparison to Kerala. In the state of Kerala the collection of taxes is comparatively high but due to high value of (devolved) funds received from government, the ratio (of total collection of taxes to total income) is low (at 10.09). As regards the annual increase of own income (of all the three tiers), it is low in most of the states, and in Kerala, Madhya Pradesh and Maharashtra, the increase is significant.

If we look at the users's charges, it is significantly low in most of the states. Its share in the total collection taxes is reasonably good in the states of Gujarat, Karnataka, Kerala and Maharashtra. While in certain states like Assam, Haryana, Meghalaya, Punjab and Uttar Pradesh the share of user's charges is nil.

Devolution of Funds: Article 243 G defines that the states may endow the panchayats with necessary powers and responsibilities for certain functions in order to enable panchayats to function as institutions of self-government and Article 243H stipulates for grant-in-aid. While except Kerala no other state has taken concrete measures to devolve funds upon panchayats in order to enable them to plan and implement the projects as per the local felt-needs.

In Kerala, at the gram panchayat level in the study area, the per capita devolution of funds is Rs. 252.52 and as percentage of total income it is 63.85. The same figure in other states is nil.

SFC: As per Article 2431 the states shall constitute state finance commission (SFC). The SFCs of almost all the states have submitted reports, still not much action has been taken to address the problem of panchayat finances. And no serious attempt has been made by the states to devolve funds upon panchayats to augment their own income. If we examine the salient recommendations, these mainly pertain to the transfer of taxes, imposition of certain taxes, besides examining in general about panchayat finances. They have not looked into certain vital points such as requirement of development funds for panchayats, based on their needs how the resources to be raised by the panchayats or devolved by the state, minimum user charges, cross subsidy, tax collection mechanism and the measures for reducing horizontal and vertical imbalances. Although, in this regard, some recommendations have been made but they are not comprehensive.

Financial Autonomy of Gram Panchayat: As regards the financial autonomy, it is very badly restricted as the grants mainly given to gram panchayats, are in the tied-form. The funds (own income and devolved funds) over which the panchayats have rights to spend as per their own plans are very less in all the states except in Kerala, where per capita availability with the panchayats is Rs. 310.02 (57.50 + 252.52), the same varies from Rs. 1.25 to Rs. 67.50 in all the other states (while as per table in the state of Haryana the own income is very high, it is basically an exception, as explained in the footnote). Thus, the low availability, coupled with tied form of grants, makes it difficult for the panchayats to exercise their financial autonomy for the projects of local importance.

Self-government Role

Table 3.12 summarizes the findings as presented above under the four dimensions of decentralization. It also reflects that the panchayats have been denied the role of self-government, as per Article 243G. The panchayats have not been given autonomy under political, functional, administrative and financial spheres. They lack political autonomy due to government control over panchayats and untimely elections. As the functions have not been transferred to panchayats, the functional autonomy has suffered. Likewise, due to inadequate administrative arrangements for empowering panchayats with powers and support system (manpower, infrastructure, etc.), the administrative autonomy is affected. The insignificant devolution of funds upon panchayats has impacted on their financial autonomy. Besides, low tax-base of panchayats and low capacity of panchayats to raise taxes have further affected their own resources.

Implementation of Scheduled Areas Act

The contents of the Act reflect that the panchayats in the Scheduled Areas are expected to perform broadly development and regulatory roles. Besides, it is assumed that the panchayats would play the self-government role with the devolution of powers upon them.

Development Role

It pertains to approval and implementation of the plans, programmes and projects for socio-economic development, identifications as well as selection of beneficiaries of poverty alleviation and other programmes, providing certification of utilization of funds and control (clause 'm') over institutions and functionaries in all social sectors as also over local plans and resources for such plans including tribal sub-plans.

Regulatory Role (Consultative and Recommendatory Role)

It (as per clause 'm') pertains to enforcement prohibition of any intoxicant, ownership of minor forest produce, prevention of alienation of land; and to manage village markets and money lending. Similarly, regarding the acquisition of land, the Act has assigned consultative power to the gram sabha. For mining lease and grant of concession for the exploitation of minor minerals, the gram sabha has been given recommendatory role.

Self-government Role

The clause 'm' states that 'while endowing panchayats in the Scheduled Areas with such powers and authority as may be necessary to enable them to function as institutions of self-government.

Critical Observations

The Same Body Exercising both Development and Regulatory Functions: Under the existing Act for Scheduled Areas, the panchayats will have to attend to both the roles viz., development and regulatory. In this context the following observations need to be taken into consideration:

The studies have indicated (field studies of Orissa, Madhya Pradesh and Maharashtra) that panchayats in the scheduled areas are marked with features like: *first*, insignificant participation of people in the gram sabha; *second*, lack of awareness in the people and poor capabilities among the panchayat members; and *third*, poor capacities of the panchayats and delivery system to handle the basic functions of development. Besides, the availability of basic services like primary education, health or drinking water is highly questionable, and due to lack of support from states the panchayats are not able to attend to these very functions up to any satisfactory level. Moreover, the public awareness and action for such needs is not visible.

To conclude, when the panchayats are not equipped to handle the basic functions, which are very vital for people, we need to re-examine the issues of burdening them with too many regulatory functions. Also, there is a danger that if the panchayats look into regulatory job, the development may not be in the desired way, not only due to their poor capacities to handle so many functions but also from the point of view of different perspective and approach attached to these two categories viz., 'development' and 'regulation'. Moreover, it is important to appreciate that we need to see the role of panchayats from the development perspective. With this kind

Table 3.12. Analysis of Panchayati Raj System

S.No.	*Dimensions*	*Items*	*Issues*	*Desired outcome (assumed)*	*Present status*	*Missing links*
1	*2*	*3*	*4*	*5*	*6*	*7*
1.	Political	• Political status	Executive position to PR members	– PR members to be given executive status	– Executive position given	–
		• Election	Timely, free and fair elections	– Timely elections every five years will be held – Free and fair elections – Representation to wider sections – Village development needs will be covered in the election campaign	– Elections held. But delayed in Assam and Bihar for a long period and also in Andhra Pradesh, Gujarat Madhya Pradesh, Karnataka and Punjab – Elections marked with undesirable activities like use of more money and liquor, and also of violence in some cases. – Influential people dominate the	Election reforms lacking

...(Contd.)

1	2	3	4	5	6	7
					election process. Facilitating the political groups to expand their base. – Issues for discussion during elections are very limited and normally, the village development needs do not form the part of it.	
		• People's participation	Attendance in the gram sabha	– People will attend the meeting in large number and participate in village development planning	– People do not attend meetings regularly and the attendance in the gram sabha is low.	– Lack of education and awareness
		• Functioning of gram sabha	People's needs and aspirations, and preparation of	– The gram sabha will be able to address the	– The gram sabha is not able to attend to people's	– Disparities due to caste, class or gender affect

...(Contd.)

1	2	3	4	5	6	7
			village plan	people's problems and will prepare the village plan	problems adequately. It lacks transparency and is dominated by a few individuals.	participation – Lack of environment building. – Proper rules and procedure for functioning of gram sabha are lacking.
		• Accountability	Accountability of PR members to people	– PR members will deliver the desired results and will be accountable to people	– There is no well-defined accountability norm and the PR members are not accountable in any form for practical purposes	– Proper procedure and awareness among people for social audit are lacking.
2.	Functional	• Transfer of functions	Transferring functions	– It will follow after the enactment of new panchayat Act	– Functions under most of the subjects are not transferred	– Lack of initiative by the departments at the state and centre levels

...(Contd.)

1	2	3	4	5	6	7
		• Assigning function specific responsibilities	Giving responsibilities to panchayats for a particular function	– It was assumed that it will follow after the enactment of new panchayat Acts in the states	– Responsibilities are not clearly defined and there is confusion over the role of PRIs at the three tiers, and also between PRIs and departments	– Lack of appreciation for defining responsibilities
		• Inter-tier demarcation of functions	Demarcating sub-function under each subject for each tier	– It will follow after the enactment of new panchayat Act	– Demarcation not carried out in order to define clear responsibilities for each tier. There are overlapping areas of functioning among panchayats, resulting in confusion and conflicts	– Lack of appreciation for the need of demarcation of functions
3.	Administrative	• Planning – Planning unit	Planning system	– People and the PR members at the village level	– Panchayats are unable to prepare plans due to poor	– Various components for planning not

...(Contd.)

1	2	3	4	5	6	7
		– Planning methodology – Database – DPC		will be able to prepare plans	people's participation, lack of knowledge and skills, and lack of support system	placed with the panchayats.
				– DPC will be formed	– Functionaries are not provided training for local level planning	– Moreover, there is a lack of appreciation for such needs (of planning)
					– DPC not formed in all the states, and it has many deficiencies and is handicapped to take up the task of district planning	– State governments have not taken measures for deputation of officers and staff
		• Placement of officers and staff of line departments with PRIs	Administrative control over officers and staff	– Panchayats will have administrative powers	– Officers and staff are not placed with the panchayats and so they are not able to perform their duties	– No provision for strengthening the support system is made

...(Contd.)

1	2	3	4	5	6	7
		• Infrastructural and logistics support	Support system	– Panchayats will be able to deliver goods to people	– Support systems is not provided to panchayats that is a big handicap for them	– Lack of awareness among people to question about the decision-making and inadequate provisions for observing transparency
		• Transparency	Transparency procedure	– Panchayats will provide scope for cpenness regarding the decision-making, and thus ensure transparency in the functioning	– Decision-making is marked with lack of openness and even the gram sabha's decisions are not transparent	– Proper measures not taken for defining responsibilities and the process for planning, implementation, coordination and monitoring
		• Institutional mechanism for planning, implementation, coordination and monitoring – Planning process and	Institutional mechanism for the preparation of development plans and the implementation of works	– Panchayats will be able to perform their functions after they are constituted	– In the absence of proper procedure, the plans are not properly prepared and people's participation remains poor, and also not	– Beneficiaries' participation in the development process is not appreciated

...(Contd.)

1	2	3	4	5	6	7
		responsibilities – Implementation process and responsibilities – Coordination with different departments – Monitoring of progress of works			implemented by involving beneficiaries. It is the chairperson of the GP who undertakes the implementation of work – For want of training, functionaries lack requisite knowledge and skills for undertaking the task of village planning and implementation of programmes	
4.	Financial	• Collection of taxes	Identification of items for taxes	– Panchayats will improve their internal resources through tax collection	– Own income of panchayats remains very low and there is a lack of initiatives by the panchayats for augmenting their income	– Panchayats lack political will to impose taxes.

...(Contd.)

1	2	3	4	5	6	7
					through collection of taxes and users charges – Tax collection mechanism poor	
		• Devolution of funds	Devolution of funds	– Panchayuats will be able to deliver results for all development activities	– Panchayats have very little resources and the devolution of funds is insignificant	– State governments have not taken steps to devolve funds upon panchayats
		• Expenditure as per its own needs	Financial autonomy to panchayats	– Panchayats will be ablve to plan and spend as pr their local need	– Panchayats virtually have no financial autonomy	– In the absence of devolution of funds, the panchayats' autonomy is affected

Note: The above observations are with respect to all the states except Kerala, the table may be referred to for comparison of status in Kerala vis-à-vis other states.

of existing framework in which the gram panchayats will be handling both development and regulatory functions, the development is going to take backseat. No doubt, the regulatory functions are very essential, but these are to be handled by a separate body.

Envisaging the Self-government Role in the Absence of Capacity Building: It is envisaged that the panchayats should function as units of self-governance. By assuming this role it enlarges their function enormously. If we examine this aspect carefully, it will require handling of political, fiscal, and administrative subjects besides legislative roles (as per definition of self-government). Now this aspect should be looked in the light of two important points: *first*, what is the present capacity of local institutions, whether they are in a position to manage such responsibility; and *second*, what is the core responsibility of panchayats, which is undoubtedly the development. These two points should be borne in mind, while deciding the functional role of panchayats. And by assigning panchayats the role of self-governance, we will be asking them to look into too many functions, which may be difficult to handle in the absence of adequate capacity.

In sum, it appears that the present Act envisages a large responsibility for the panchayats starting from village planning to implementation of plan to management of MFP and village markets to regulation of illicit liquor and money lending. With this kind of approach, there is no focused approach. Development, which should be at the centre of the panchayat system in the tribal areas, has lost prominence. And it is likely that at the functional level, when the panchayats will start devoting their time and resources on regulation, the development of areas is further going to suffer. Moreover, experience shows that development and regulation require different approaches and cannot go hand in hand, so the efficiency of panchayats functioning, especially in respect of development, is bound to suffer. Besides, the following questions remain unanswered:

- *first*, what is not logical is as to why to give the dual responsibility (of regulation and development) to panchayats while both the functions require altogether different approach; and

- *second*, why the primacy of development has not been realized while the tribal areas with low HRD and infrastructural level require more focus on these issues.

No Power to Gram Sabha for Development Projects under Forest Land: As most of the tribal areas fall under forest areas (reserve or protected), so in the villages it becomes difficult to locate suitable land for development projects especially for check-dams or irrigation structures. It causes problems at the time of implementation of projects, and due to non-availability of suitable land, either projects get delayed or are not executed. But to handle this problem, which is very common in tribal areas, there is no power given to gram sabha in the Act.

Other Vital Issues

Observations from the People's Perspective

The major objective of the panchayati raj system has been to give opportunities to people to participate in the decision-making of the development process so that the grassroots problems can be reflected in the village development plans. Or, in other words, it was envisaged that the people would be given central position in the village development planning and implementation. But if we examine the observations made by the people during the field studies, the following points emerge:

Wide Disparities among People: There is wide disparity among people on the basis of caste or income or property or affiliation to political party, which creates divisions among society. And in the absence of any proper corrective measure through sustained educational and economic programmes, the disparity continues to widen gap in some cases or marginalize the underpriveleged section in some other. Environment for participation remains indifferent, passive and sometimes hostile. Such a state of village society is highly detrimental for the decentralization process and needs urgent attention inorder to involve people meanginfully in the village development. And without attending this vital issue the participatory development would remain a remote possibility.

Individuals are not Valued: Due to inherent tendency of central decision-making (existing political culture) and the tendency to project one's supremacy by PR members and elites, the individual's abilities are not given importance. The views of the individuals do not matter, and thus the possibility of participation as well as contribution by them in blocked.

Institutions are Inaccessible to People: In the absence of support system, local institutions do not attend to the basic needs of the people and fail to instill confidence in them.

Inadequacy of Proper Rules and Management: The present PR system does not give importance to rules and procedures, as also it fails to recognize the need of management and professional approach for development and making basic services available to people. Thus, it puts the people on periphery as those who are manning the institutions can get away without following the norms and attending to the genuine needs of people.

Powers to Village Elites with little Accountability: Facilitating the political parties to get power, without accountability, in the absence of proper institutional mechanism.

Presently, with more focus on elections and certain other provisions on reservation, devolution of powers, etc., it appears that the PR system is assumed more as a political entity and of a source of power, rather than a means of providing services to people. In operational terms, there is a clear lack of vision as to how the people will get opportunities to participate, contribute and take advantage of development. Mere provisions on gram sabhas, or elections, or reservations, or devolution of powers, though important, will not be enough for the people to participate, in the absence of conducive as well as enabling environment and without institutional development.

Institutional Performance

Institutional role is vital in the development process, which will include planning of resources, implementation of

Table 3.13. Factors affecting Institutional Performance at the Panchayat Level

S.No.	*Component*	*Factors affecting Institutional Performance*	*Impact*
1	*2*	*3*	*4*
1.	Institutional processes	– Inadequate procedure – Lack of transparency – No accountability of elected representatives	– Lack of direction for the functioning. Sometimes it causes confusion – Loss of papers and documents, which causes distrust – Decisions taken more by personal choice than by rational approach – The elected members are not accountable to people, so whatever members do there is a lack of control over that. There are instances of aberrations.
2.	HRD level of personnel	– Lack of technical, administrative and behavioural capabilities	– Personnel are not able to plan and implement programmes properly
3.	Financial system	– Poor financial base – Inadequate tax collection mechanism	– Lack of financial capacity and autonomy – Panchayats are unable to plan as per their local needs
4.	Planning	– Inadequate planning unit – No proper process and procedure of planning	– The planning of resources is an *ad hoc* basis, without following rational basis

...(Contd.)

5.	Management of implementation	– Lack of manpower and logistics planning – Poor infrastructural support – Inadequate management capabilities – Weak information system	– Management of implementation of works and the availability of services to people gets seriously affected
6.	Control and Monitoring	– Inadequate control and monitoring system	– Projects are not properly monitored. – Financial position of the panchayat income and resources are not known in time.
7.	Legal system	– Weak mechanism to settle disputes and aberrations in decision-making	– There are inter-group conflicts, that disrupt the panchayat functioning and the implementation of works gets delayed – No check over aberrations or excess of power/control

programmes, monitoring and control, legal framework and making services available to people. A careful examination of factors responsible for institutional performance reveals how panchayats at the district, block and gram panchayat levels are incapacitated to perform. Some of the salient drawbacks are as follows:

To begin with, we take the case of *institutional processes*. It is marked with lack of procedures and norms for the conduct of gram sabha, transparency and accountability, planning and implementation of programmes. The work goes on without following systematic process, which results into confusion, loss of papers and documents, distrust, and so on. As regards the HRD level of personnel of PR institutions, it seems to be the last priority, as if the planning and implementation of programmes can be handled without knowledge and skills. Here it is pertinent to mention that the functionaries are not properly equipped to handle the task of development due to lack of requisite technical, administrative and behavioural capabilities. They do not have skills for local level planning, management abilities to provide services to people and the capabilities to work with and for the people. As for the financial system, it is handicapped by lack of resources, weak tax collection mechanism and inadequate procedure for finance and accounts. Regarding the issues of planning system, it is not placed in the desired manner of handling the task of participatory micro/ district planning. Similarly, management of implementation suffers due to poor managerial abilities of functionaries and the lack of emphasis on involvement of beneficiaries in the implementation process. Likewise, monitoring and control of programme implementation suffer due to inadequate mechanism and the inabilities of functionaries. And, finally, the legal system is completely missing to address the disputes, which quite often arise.

It appears that, in the absence of vital fundamentals, the straightening of local institutions is largely ignored or dealt with superficially. In practice, capacity-building of PR institutions remains a big cause of concern. The studies illustrate the infancy of the institutional development at the local levels.

In this backdrop, it is amply clear that the local institutions cannot be in a position to address the development needs and to meet the aspirations of people. It is simply assumed that panchayat Acts, though vital, would automatically lead to greater institutional capability. And simply conducting elections or extending powers will do very little, in the absence of adequate institutional support.

Salient Observations of Process of Decentralization in the State of Kerala

Under people's campaign plan, the state government initiated several measures for decentralizing the development process from district to gram panchayat level. The salient points are presented below:

Environmental Building: In order to create conducive environment for the participation of people, instilling confidence in them and also for giving a sense of responsibility to PR members about the village development, the state took steps for building environment in villages. Under this programme, a number of activities such as distribution of literature on development issues, display of development activities through posters and charts, cultural programmes and orientation and training programmes were organized. The programme of environment building gave confidence to people and PR members that they can undertake the works of village development.

People's Participation: A special emphasis has been given to ensure people's participation in the gram sabha, in the decision-making process of development planning, as also in the implementation and supervision of programmes. For ensuring people's attendance in the gram sabha, activities like door-to-door contact programme, announcement in the villages and on radio, etc., have been taken up. Besides, development seminars at the gram panchayat level are organized. It has resulted in achieving four objectives: *first*, high attendance in the gram sabha; *second*, active participation in the discussion; *third,* collection of information on local problems and resources; and *fourth,* increased responsiveness of PR members for the problems of people and villages.

Institution Building: Government has initiated measures for institution building at all the three tiers. Infrastructural and logistics support has been added. The field officers and staff of line departments have been deputed to panchayats, which have been given working administrative powers. Also, these functionaries have been given training on local level planning, behavioural skills (to work with people and PR members), project formulation, implementation of works, and so on. Transfer of functions, inter-tier demarcation of functions and devolution of funds upon panchayats have taken place. In a way, necessary functional, administrative and financial responsibilities and powers have been placed with the panchayats alongwith adequate support system that has provided good strength to the local institutions to perform their duties.

Devolution of Funds: The government has taken steps for devolving funds upon panchayats at all the three tiers. The funds are directly placed with the three tiers by the government. The devolution of funds was started in 1997-98 and 36 per cent of the state plan budget was earmarked for the municipalities and panchayats. Among panchayats, the gram panchayats were given bigger share in comparison to other two tiers. Under general sector, it was distributed to the gram panchayats, block panchayats and district panchayats in the ratio of 70:15:15. The devolution has improved the financial base of the panchayats significantly and resulted in providing financial autonomy to them in order to enable them to utilize funds as per local needs.

Planning: In order to make rational allocation of funds, a special drive has been undertaken for participatory planning. Under this, the elaborate guidelines and methodology for planning have been formulated. It includes a number of steps: *first,* defining planning process at the gram sabha and gram panchayat levels; *second*, formation of technical corps (groups) for giving technical inputs; *third*, database preparation and technical discussion about data analysis, backward and forward linkages analysis, inter-sectoral analysis, feasibility studies, project formulation, and so on; *fourth*, project appraisal; *fifth*, finalization of plan document at gram panchayat level; and *finally*, integration of gram panchayat plans with the block and district plans. Also, comprehensive training programmes for PR members and development functionaries were organized all over the state in order to equip them with necessary knowledge and skills for planning.

Implementation of Programmes: Similarly, a detailed procedure for the implementation of works has been prescribed. It includes formation of beneficiaries committee, training of representatives of committee, supervision of quality of works by the beneficiaries, check-measurement procedure and monitoring of the progress of work.

System of Transparency and Accountability: In order to make people aware and to make panchayat functioning open, various steps have been taken for ensuring transparency in the functioning of panchayats. Some of them are display of accounts outside the gram panchayat office, disclosure of accounts in the gram sabha meeting, availability of proceedings of gram sabha and gram panchayat meetings, and involvement of beneficiaries in the implementation of works. With the increasing role of PR members and their responsibilities for the work, a system of social audit has been introduced in which people can ask questions to PR members about the decisions taken by them. Besides, financial audit has been introduced for checking accounts and the appropriateness of the financial procedures. These measures have helped not only in active participation by people but also in making PR members responsive to the people's needs and in observing the functional propriety, that has resulted in improving the effectiveness of PR institutions.

Overall, the measures initiated by the government in Kerala have led to good working environment, which has led to increase in demands from the people for their village development and has also provided opportunities to PR institutions to deliver goods. Finally, it has facilitated in improving the efficiency and effectiveness of local institutions in addressing the local development needs and aspirations of people.

In a nutshell, in Kerala, unlike other states, the fundamentals are rightly placed and the comparative analysis is presented in Table 3.14. The state has given primacy to people's participation in a meaningful way and to developing capabilities of people at large and of PR members in particular. Genuine efforts have been made for institution building in terms of infrastructural, manpower, administrative and financial support. Initiatives have been taken for encouraging transparency in the functioning and for the accountability of elected representatives to people.

However, from the point of view of H sustainability of decentralization process, the support from the state government is vital and should be on a sustained basis. Also, some aberrations that take place with regard to beneficiaries' selection, or engagement of proxy contractors for implementation of work, or inadequacy of social audit, need to be watched carefully and appropriate action needs to be taken for rectifying defects or improving procedures. And the overall spirit of decentralized governance that has been generated by people's plan campaign (PPC) should be sustained and further strengthened.

Indicators Analysis

Analysis of Pre-requisites for Decentralization

There are certain vital pre-requisites (Manor, 1999), which need to be placed at the local levels, before any process of decentralization should begin. These pre-requisites are:

- Environment building: suitable behavioural and psychological factors;

Table 3.14. A Comparative Picture of Status of System of Decentralization in Kerala and other States

S.No.	*Elements*	*Status in Kerala*	*Status in other states*
1	2	3	4
1.	**Political Decentralization**		
	Environment building	– Awareness building and training programmes at panchayat level	– No special efforts for environment building
	People's participation	– Improved attendance in gramsabhas. Active participation by people due to better educational awareness.	– Poor people's participation
	Role of PR members	– Active involvement by PR members due to their higher educational background, and improved knowledge and skills through training programmes	– Little interaction of PR members with people in development matters – Lack of initiative by the PR members for development activities
	Role of gram sabha	– High attendance. Active participation by the PR members and people	– Low attendance – Dominance by a few people
2.	**Functional Decentralization**		
	Transfer of functions	– Transfer of functions for all the subjects has taken place – Also inter-tier demarcation of functions has taken place	– Transfer of functions has not been complete

...(Contd.)

1	2	3	4
3.	**Administrative Decentralization**		
	Capacity building	– Well-organized training programme at all the three tiers. Close monitoring of programmes by the government	– Only a few programmes at concerned SIRDs but no comprehensive training programme
	Infrastructure	– Good infrastructure with gram panchayats	– Insufficient infrastructure
	Manpower support	– Good number of staff. Placement of staff and officers of other departments with gram/block / district panchayat	– Skeleton staff
	Planning		
	i. Planning unit	– Existing	– Partially existing
	ii. Database	– Prepared for each sector at GP, block and district	– Database not developed
	iii. Planning methodology		
	a. Procedure of planning	– Well-laid out procedure for planning at each tier	– No procedure developed
	b. Planning team at GP, block, and district	– Full-fledged planning team with experts.	– No earmarked team – No earmarked team
	c. Technical team		– No earmarked team
	d. Appraisal team	– Formed at block and district	– Not constituted in some states
	e. District planning committee	– Formed at block and district	– No attention is given
	f. Project formulation	– DPC constituted	– Functions not clearly demarcated
	g. Functions for each tier		– No procedure prepared

...(*Contd.*)

1	2	3	4
	h. Integrated of GP plan with higher tiers	– Proper procedure and techniques developed – Clearly demarcated functions for each tier with regard to all – Well-defined procedure	
4.	**Financial Decentralization**		
	Devolution of funds	– About 40% of state plan devolved upon panchayats	– No devolution of funds
5.	**Overall Measures**		
	Role of Government	– People's plan campaign launched which resulted into higher people's participation – Transfer of functions and devolution of financial powers upon panchayats	– No specific plan for strengthening participatory planning – No devolution of financial power

- Sufficient powers to exercise substantial influence within the political system and over significant development activities;
- Sufficient financial resources to accomplish important tasks;
- Adequate administrative capacity to accomplish those tasks; and
- Reliable accountability mechanisms—to ensure both the accountability of elected politicians to citizens and the accountability of government officials to elected politicians.

Under each of the identified pre-requisites, the analysis for assessing the status of pre-requisites is carried out as per the specific initiatives taken by the states and the points have been given to each state.

- ***Under Political Decentralization***

Political Devolution: The states have made suitable provisions in their panchayat Acts for timely election and giving executive position to the chairpersons of three-tiers.

Environment Building: Suitable Behavioural and Psychological Factors: Environment building is vital for providing a suitable environment for decentralization so that the people can participate freely and actively. The state of Kerala has taken special measures under people's plan campaign in which awareness building activities like cultural shows, village meetings, door-to-door campaign, dissemination of information through visual and print media, etc., were organized. Also, under sensitization programme, training programmes for PR members and other field officers and staff were organized at all the three tiers in a comprehensive manner. While in other states some efforts have been made partially for awareness building.

Reliable Accountability Mechanisms to ensure both the Accountability of Elected Politicians to Citizens and the Accountability of Government Officials to Elected Politicians:

Though the states have made an attempt to ensure accountability, yet it has not been ensured fully in most of the states, except Kerala. As regards social audit, the government in Kerala has given orders and framed guidelines for it and the people have been made aware. In other states, some provisions have been made in the Act but necessary awareness among people has not been duly ensured. Regarding the accountability of officials to PR members, some steps, in terms of writing of ACRs of officers of line departments, have been taken in Kerala and the states under category B.

- ***Under Functional Decentralization***

Sufficient Powers to Exercise Substantial Influence within the Political System and over Significant Development Activities (transfer of functions): In order to provide the functional support to panchayats, the Kerala government has taken initiatives for transfer of functions to panchayats and also for demarcation of functions among three tiers. Whereas other states have taken some steps for transferring partially the functions to panchayats, but no concrete steps have been taken to demarcate the functions among three tiers.

- ***Under Administrative Decentralization***

Adequate Administrative Capacity to accomplish Tasks: In Kerala the steps have been taken by the government to transfer the services of field officers and staff of several departments at three tiers. The planning unit has been partially set up in terms of facility for database preparation, formulation of planning methodology and the planning process, and training to field officers and staff. Still, there is a need for creating infrastructure and providing equipments at all the three tiers. In other states, the transfer of field officers and staff to panchayat levels has not taken place, and also planning units have not been set up. In the states of Maharashtra and Karnataka, under the category B, only a few officers and staff have been placed partially with the zilla parishad.

Similarly, in the state of Kerala the measures have been taken to provide infrastructural and logistics support and to impart training to field officers and staff for various development programmes. As regards the transparency, it has been ensured by the Act and also measures have been taken to ensure its implementations by way of increasing public awareness. While other states are lacking in these areas.

- ***Under Financial Decentralization***

Sufficient Financial Resources to accomplish Important Tasks: Kerala has taken concrete measure for devolving funds upon panchayats from the state plan. In the states of Gujarat, Karnataka and Maharashtra, funds are placed with the zilla parishad, but these are earmarked for certain schemes. But in other states there was no devolution of funds. With regard to setting up of system for financial management and accounting, it is not fully set up in all the states.

Based on the points secured, the states (about prerequisites) have been classified as under:

Category A : Kerala

Category B : Gujarat, Karnataka, Maharashtra and West Bengal

Category C : Andhra Pradesh, Assam, Haryana, Madhya Pradesh, Punjab, Orissa, Rajasthan, Tamil Nadu and Uttar Pradesh

In sum, non of the states, except Kerala, have tried to place pre-requisites for decentralization, while operationalizing their respective Panchayat Acts. The efforts for creating conducive environment have not been made in order to prepare people especially from weaker sections to participate in local village development. There are various behavioural (due to gender and/or inter-class or inter-personal relationship) and psychological (mind-set, inertia) factors that have bearing on the way people interact and participate, but attempts are not made to bring attitudinal changes to create

Table 3.15. Analysis of Status of Prerequisites for Decentralization – Procedure of Points

Prerequisites	*Indicators*	*Present status*	*Points*	*Category A*	*Category B*	*Category C*
1	*2*	*3*	*4*	*5*	*6*	*7*
Political Decentralization Political Devolution	– Timely election	(i) Timely election (ii) Untimely (iii) Not at all	1 .5 0	Timely election provided by the Act	Timely election provided by the Act	Timely election provided by the Act
	– Political status to chairpersons of panchayats	(i) Provided by the Act (ii) Not provided	1 0	Provided by the Act Very good	Provided by the Act Good	Provided by the Act Average
Environment building: suitable behavioural and psychological factors	– Orientation workshop in the villages	(i) Very good (ii) Good (iii) Average	1 .5 0	Organized	Partially organized	Partially organized
	– Training for attitudinal changes among PR members & field officers and staff	(i) Organized (ii) Partially (iii) Not organized	1 .5 0	Fully done	Partially done	Partially done
	– Distribution of literature among	(i) Fully done (ii) Partially done	1 .5	Fully provided	Partially provided (Only general purpose training)	Partially provided

...(*Contd.*)

1	2	3	4	5	6	7
	villagers and conduct of gram sabha	(iii) Not done	0			
	– Training to PR members for basic subjects	(i) Fully provided (ii) Partially provided (iii) Not provided	1 .5 0			
Reliable accountability mechanisms to ensure both the accountability of elected politicians to citizens, and the accountability of government officials to elected politicians	– Accountability system with proper procedure (including social audit)	(i) Full (ii) Partial (iii) Not done	1 .5 0	Partial (but significant steps)	Partial	Partial
	– Accountability of government officials to elected representative	(i) Full (ii) Partial (iii) Not done	1 .5 0	Partial	Partial	Not done
Functional Decentralization– Sufficient	– Transfer of functions in	(i) Full (ii) Partial	1 .5	Full	Partial	Partial

...(*Contd.*)

1	2	3	4	5	6	7
powers to exercise substantial influence within the political system and over significant development activities (transfer of functions)	each subject	(iii) Not done	0			
	– Subject-wise demarcation of functions at each tier	(i) Full (ii) Partial (iii) Not done	1 .5 0	Full	Not done	Not done
Administrative– Decentralization Adequate administrative capacity to accomplish tasks	Placement of field officers & staff with each tier	(i) Full (ii) Partial (iii) Not done	1 .5 0	Partial	Not done (in Karnataka and Maharashtra, some staff deputed to ZP)	Not done
	– Planning unit at each tier	(i) Set up fully (ii) Partial set-up (iii) No set-up	1 .5 0	Partial set-up	Not set-up	No set-up
	– Training to field officers and staff for planning and implementation	(i) Fully orgnaized (ii) Partially organized (iii) Not organized	1 .5 0	Fully organized	Partially organized	Not organized
	– Infrastructural support	(i) Fully provided	1	Fully provided	Partial	Little support

...(Contd.)

1	2	3	4	5	6	7
	for office, training centre, etc.	(ii) Partial (iii) Little support	.5 0			
	– Logistics support	(i) Fully provided (ii) Partial (iii) Little support	1 .5 0	Fully provided	Partial	Little support
	– Transparency system	(i) Full (ii) Partial (iii) Not done	1 .5 0	Full	Partial	Partial
Financial Decentralization Sufficient financial resources to accomplish important tasks	– Financial management and accounting system	(i) Set-up (ii) Partial set-up (iii) No set-up	1 .5 0	Partial set-up	Partial set-up	Partial set-up
	– Devolution of funds	(i) Full (ii) Partial (iii) Not done	1 .5 0	Full	Partial	Not done

Prerequisites

Category A – Kerala

Category B states – Gujarat, Karnataka, Maharashtra and West Bengal

Category C states – Andhra Pradesh, Assam, Haryana, Madhya Pradesh, Punjab, Orissa, Rajasthan, Tamil Nadu and Uttar Pradesh

Table 3.16. Summary of Points achieved by Different States for placing Prerequisities for Decentralization

S.No.	Category	Name of the State	Points for Pre-requisite							
			Political decentralization			Functional decentra-lization	Adminis-trative decentra-lization	Financial decentra-lization	Total points	Achieve-ment as % of total points
			Political	Environ-mental building	Accounta-bility	Transfer of functions	Capacity to function	Financial system and devolution of funds		
1.	A	Kerala	2.0	4.0	1.0	2	5.0	1.5	15.5	86.11
2.	B	Gujarat	2.0	2.0	1.0	.5	2.0	1.0	8.5	47.22
3.		Karnataka	2.0	2.0	1.0	.5	2.5	1.0	9.0	50.00
4.		Maharashtra	2.0	2.0	1.0	.5	2.5	1.0	9.0	50.00
5.		West Bengal	2.0	2.0	1.0	.5	2.0	1.0	8.5	47.22
6.	C	Andhra Pradesh	2.0	1.5	5	.5	.5	.5	5.5	30.55
7.		Assam	NA	-	-	-	-	-	-	-
8.		Haryana	2.0	1.5	5	.5	.5	.5	5.5	30.55
9.		Madhya Pradesh	2.0	1.5	5	.5	.5	.5	5.5	30.55
10.		Meghalaya	NA	-	-	-	-	-	-	-
11.		Punjab	2.0	1.5	5	.5	.5	.5	5.5	30.55
12.		Orissa	2.0	1.5	5	.5	.5	.5	5.5	30.55
13.		Rajasthan	2.0	1.5	5	.5	.5	.5	5.5	30.55
14.		Tamil Nadu	2.0	1.5	5	.5	.5	.5	5.5	30.55
15.		Uttar Pradesh	2.0	1.5	5	.5	.5	.5	5.5	30.55

...(Contd.)

favourable factors for participation in the local development. Apart from these, the steps for transferring functions, and enhancing administrative capacity and financial resources together with accountability mechanism have not been taken as pre-requisites to enable panchayats to function as institutions of self-government.

Finally, if we look at the summary of the points that are given to different states in Table 3.16, Kerala has got 15.5 points, which is 86.11 per cent of the total points, and the states under category B have got between 8.5 and 9.0 points, indicating 47.22 per cent to 50.00 per cent of the efforts required for placing pre-requisites. And the points secured by the states under category C are 5.5, which is 30.55 per cent of the desired efforts for decentralization. The analysis reflects that in Kerala more than eighty per cent (86.11) of the required efforts were made to place pre-requisites in the desired shape at the local levels.

Analysis of Present Status of PR System

The findings in this section are analysed based on the field study and survey conducted, the salient point are listed below:

- ***Under Political Decentralization***

Timely Elections: Most of the states have conducted their panchayat elections in time but in the states of Andhra Pradesh, Karnataka and Madhya Pradesh, the elections were delayed, and in the states of Punjab and Gujarat they have been postponed. In case of Assam elections were held after a gap of nine years.

Political Position: All the states have provided the necessary political positions to elected representatives at all the three tiers.

Environment in the Panchayats: For assessing the environment in the panchayats the issues considered are: socio-political environment, people's participation and participation of officials and staff.

Table 3.17. Measuring the Efficacy of Present Status of PR System – Procedure for points

S.N.	Item	Issues	Indicator	Status	Points	Category A	Category B	Category C
1	2	3	4	5	6	7	8	9
1.	Political Decentralization	Election	(a) Timely election	(i) Timely election (ii) Untimely (iii) Not at all	1 .5 0	Timely election	Timely election (but not in Gujarat, Karnataka and Punjab)	Timely election (But not in A.P. and M.P., and not held in Assam till 2000)
		Political devolution	(b) Political position	(i) Provided by the Act (ii) Not provided	+1 –1	Provided by the Act	Provided by the Act (term for the chairpersons deduced in Karnataka and Maharashtra)	Provided by the Act
	Environment in the panchayat	Social-political environment	(a) Socio-politico groups	(i) Supportive (ii) Neutral (iii) Warring groups	+1 0 –1	Supportive	Normal	Normal (Warring groups in case of UP)
		People's participation	(a) Attitude of people	(i) Supportive (ii) Normal (passive) (iii) Negative	+1 0 –1	Supportive	Normal (passive)	Normal (Negative in case of Up)
							Normal	Normal
	Accountability	Participation of officials and staff	(a) Attitude of officials and staff	(i) Supportive (ii) Normal (iii) Negative	+1 0 –1	Full	Full	Full
		Financial and social audit	(a) Financial audit	(i) Full system (ii) Partia (iii) No	1 .5 0	Partial	No (In Karnataka, *Jamabandi*)	No

1	2	3	4	5	6	7	8	9
			(b) Social audit at GP level	(i) Fully developed (ii) Partial (iii) No	1 .5 0	Full	Partial	Partial
2.	**Functional Decentralization**	Functions at three tiers	(a) Transfer of functions (all subjects)	(i) Full (ii) Partial (iii) No	1 .5 0	Full	Partial	Partial
			(b) Transfer of functions upon panchayats for basic	(i) Full (ii) Partial (iii) No	1 .5 0	High	Medium	Low
3.	**Adminis-trative Decentrali-zation**	People's capacity	(a) Literacy level (b) Awareness level	(i) High (ii) Medium (iii) Low	1 .5 0	High	Medium	Low
	Capacity of PR institutions	Capabilities of PR members	(a) Education level of PR members	(i) High (ii) Medium (iii) Low	1 .5 0	High level	Medium	Low
			(b) Ability to manage panchayat functiong	(i) High level (ii) Medium (iii) Low	1 .5 0	High	Medium	Medium
			(c) Ability to do planning	(i) High (ii) Medium (iii) Low	1 .5 0	Medium	Low	Low

...(Contd.)

1	2	3	4	5	6	7	8	9
			d. Ability to implement and monitor the programmes	(i) High (ii) Medium (iii) Low	1 .5 0	Medium	Medium	Low
		System of local level planning (at all three tiers)	a. Planning Unit	(i) Fully developed (ii) Partial (iii) Not existing	1 .5 0	Partial	Not existing	Not existing
			b. Database development facility	(i) Fully developed (ii) Partial (iii) Not existing	1 .5 0	Fully developed	Not existing	Not existing
			c. Planning methodology	(i) Formulated (ii) Partially done (iii) Not formulated (i) Full support (ii) Partial (iii) Weak	1 .5 0	Formulated	Not formulated	Not formulated
		Support system	a. Manpower	(i) Full support (ii) Partial (iii) Weak	1 .5 0	Partial	Weak	Weak
			b. Infrastructural support		1 .5 0	Full	Partial/Weak in case of Maharashtra	Weak

...(Contd.)

1	2	3	4	5	6	7	8	9
			(c) Logistics (equipments, vehicles, etc.)	(i) Fully provided (ii) Partial (iii) Not provided	1 .5 0	Partial	Partial	Weak
		Adminis-trative set-up (at all three tiers)	(a) Adminis-trative structure (control over deptt.)	(i) PRIs have full control (ii) Partial control (iii) No control	1 .5 0	Partial	No control	No control
			(b) Writing of ACRs	(i) Initiated by PR heads (ii) Partial (iii) No	1 .5 0	Partial	Partial (not in Punjab and Haryana)	No
		System of transparency and monitoring	(a) System of transparency at GP level	(i) Full system (ii) Partial (iii) No	1 .5 0	Full	Partial	Partial
			(b) System of monitoring at GP level	(i) Full system (ii) Partial (iii) No	1 .5 0	Partial	Not done	No
		Implemen-tation of programmes	(a) Implemen-tation planning	(i) Planning made (ii) Partial (iii) Not done	1 .5 0	Planning made	Not done	Not done

...(Contd.)

1	2	3	4	5	6	7	8	9
			(b) Beneficiaries' participation	(i) Good participation (ii) Partial (iii) Not involved	1 .5 0	Good participation	Not involved	Not involved
		Tax collection mechanism	Tax collection mechanism	(i) Well established (ii) Partially existing (iii) Not at all	1 .5 0	Well established	Partially existing	Partially existing
4.	**Financial Decentralization**	Financial devolution (at all three tiers)Taxation	(a) Devolution of funds	(i) Full (ii) Partial (iii) No	1 .5 0	Full	Partial (not in Punjab and Haryana)	No
			(a) Tax collection base at district level	(i) High (ii) Medium (iii) Low	1 .5 0	High	Medium (High in Punjab and Haryana but low in Karnataka, Gujarat and West Bengal)	Low (Medium in Andhra Pradesh)
			(b) Financial management	(i) Full system (ii) Partia (iii) No	1 .5 0	Full	Partial	Partial

Present status

Category A – Kerala

Category B states – Gujarat, Haryana, Karnataka, Maharashtra, Punjab and West Bengal

Category C states – Andhra Pradesh, Assam, Madhya Pradesh, Orissa, Rajasthan, Tamil Nadu and Uttar Pradesh

Note: In Kerala in spite of some aberrations, the system of planning and implementation of programmes has been very well-placed in comparison to other states. Transparency, social audit and financial management are observed satisfactorily, though there may be a need of improvement.

As per the information gathered about the indicators, it was revealed that in Kerala, there are supportive socio-political groups that have helped in the decentralization process. Also, the attitude of people and officials and staff are found to be supportive. In this state, the government has taken initiatives for creating conducive environment through awareness building programmes and training for attitudinal changes that has resulted in favourable and supportive environment for participatory planning and development. The field observations revealed that in other states the environment in the panchayat is normal which does not inspire much confidence in the process of decentralization. But the matter of particular concern is the presence of warring groups and negative attitude of several people (at the village level) in the state of Uttar Pradesh, which is having some dampening effect on the measures initiated by the state government (in 1999) for empowering the panchayats.

Accountability: The financial audit has been put in place in all the states, while in none of the states, except Kerala, the social audit has been given due importance in operational terms. Though the provisions have been made for the social audit, but in the gram sabha PR members are not very responsive for the questions raised by the people, whereas in Kerala the chairpersons of gram panchayats have to answer the questions in the gram sabha and take appropriate action if required. However, much more needs to be done to strengthen social audit in Kerala.

- ***Under Financial Decentralization***

Except in Kerala, the functions have not been fully transferred to the panchayats. Even the subjects under basic services like primary education, health, drinking water, agriculture, etc. are transferred partially in other states.

- ***Under Administrative Decentralization***

Capacity of PRIs

People's Capacity: To understand the capacity of people two parameters viz., literacy level and awareness level were identified. The observations and available information indicated that the literacy and awareness are high in the case of Kerala, while the same is medium in the states covered under category B and low under category C.

Capabilities of PR Members: For judging the capabilities of PR members the four indicators were chosen. These are: education level of PR members, ability to manage panchayat functioning, ability to do planning, and ability to implement as well as monitor the programmes. In all these indicators, Kerala's performance is much better.

System of Local Level Planning: Of particular importance was the need to assess the existing planning system at the gram panchayat level. We identified three fundamental factors: *First*, planning unit; *second*, database development facility; and *third*, planning methodology. Here also Kerala stands apart from other states and has taken concrete measures for improving the system of local level of planning.

Support System: It was of vital importance to study the support system available with the gram panchayats. For this we studied manpower, infrastructural and logistics support available at the gram panchayat level in order to enable it to implement development programmes (or deliver goods and services to people). The support system is far better placed with the gram panchayats in Kerala that has enabled them to have efficient delivery mechanism.

Administrative Set-up: Administrative set-up was studied to know the control of PRIs over the line departments. It brought out that in Kerala the PRIs have partial control over some departments viz., block, agriculture, animal husbandary, health, drinking water, ICDS and primary education. The other states do not have control over line departments for practical purposes. As regards writing of the ACRs, it is written by the chairpersons (of ZP and Block) only of CEO, ZP, BDO and officer of the line departments in the case of Kerala, while in other states of category B, ACRs of only CEO, ZP is written by the chairperson of ZP.

System of Transparency: The states have made necessary provisions for maintaining transparency either through panchayat Act or government order, and these provisions make it mandatory for the panchayats to display their accounts outside their offices and at prominent places, to disclose the accounts in the gram sabha, and to provide the certified copies to people, if demanded. But in practice, it is Kerala which has been able to successfully implement the provisions of transparency. It is due to high awareness among people, the consciousness among PR members about the need of transparency in the functioning of panchayats and constant monitoring by the state government. While in other states people are not aware and PR members are not very keen about the same.

System of Monitoring: The system of monitoring at the GP level has been partially set up in Kerala, and the necessary physical and financial status of various programmes and schemes can be monitored smoothly. In other states, the status report is not available in time and also the status is not monitored properly.

Implementation: Implementation of programmes lacks proper planning and beneficiaries' participation, except in Kerala, though it may require important additions.

Similarly, *the tax collection mechanism* is not well-established in all the states, except in Kerala.

- ***Under Financial Decentralization***

To examine the financial decentralization, broadly three parameters viz., devolution of funds, tax collection base and financial management were identified.

Devolution of Funds: In Kerala, the funds have been devolved directly upon all the three tiers. As these funds are untied (in nature), panchayats have flexibility in having the schemes suited to the local needs. Though the states like Gujarat, Karnataka, Madhya Pradesh and Maharashtra are getting funds directly from the state plans but these funds are earmarked for a particular programme/scheme and the zilla parishads in these states have virtually no flexibility of having the schemes of their choice.

Tax Collection Base: As regards the tax collection base, it has significant base in Haryana, Kerala and Punjab, whereas in other states it is very low.

Financial Management: Except in Kerala, other states are not having adequate financial management in terms of trained personnel, fund planning, maintenance of books of accounts and management of tax collection.

Based on the analysis and the points assigned to states, the following classification (of present status) of states has been made.

Category A	:	Kerala
Category B	:	Gujarat, Haryana, Karnataka, Maharashtra, Punjab and West Bengal
Category C	:	Andhra Pradesh, Assam, Madhya Pradesh, Orissa, Rajasthan, Tamil Nadu and Uttar Pradesh

Finally, the points given to different states have been summarized in Table 3.18. It shows that Kerala has got 26.5 points, which is 85.48 per cent of the total points, and the states under category B have got between 9.0 and 10.0 points with achievement level between 29.03 per cent and 34.25 per cent. But the points secured by the states under category C are very low and are between 3.5 and 6.0, signifying the achievement between 11.29 per cent and 19.35 per cent. This analysis presents a scenario which shows that all the states are lagging behind in decentralizing the development system, but only in Kerala the process of decentralization has got some direction and also has got success in operational terms.

SWOT Analysis

In the backdrop of the findings as presented above, the SWOT analysis has been carried out. The salient points are indicated below:

Strength: The Act provides constitutional status to panchayats at all the three tiers, provisions for timely elections every five years, representation to weaker sections, the scope for transfer of functions and devolution of funds upon panchayats.

Weaknesses: The PR institutions are handicapped by lack of people's abilities to participate in the village development and poor capacities of local institutions to deliver.

Opportunities: The panchayati raj system opens a whole range of opportunities for the participation of people and local institutions in the village development.

Threats: There are a number of socio-economic and cultural factors such as disparities, dominance by village elites, resistance by existing political and government set-up, etc., that pose threat to the growth of local institutions and the process of decentralization.

How the Present System is an Extension of the Previous System : inadequacy of Governance

An attempt is made to draw a comparison between what existed before 1992 and what changes have occurred thereafter, as regards the implementation of the 73rd Amendment Act. A careful look at table shows that even after the new Amendment Act, there has not been perceptible difference in achieving the objectives of decentralization and in providing good governance at the grassroots level. The specific points are summed up as follows:

- Firstly, we look *from the point of view of representation of people in the panchayat set-up*. It is amply evident that the traditional elites and political groups hold sway over others. Weaker sections do not get support and the voice in the panchayat functioning. Moreover, the reservation remains confined only to the reserved seats and that too mainly for the election purpose. During elections, the environment remains politically surcharged and overwhelming, and thus highly

Table 3.18. Summary of Points for Present Status of PR System in different States

S.No.	Category	Name of the State	Points for Prerequisite						Total points	Achievement as % of total points
			Political decentralization			Functional decentralization	Administrative decentralization	Financial decentralization		
			Political	Environmental building	Accountability	Transfer of functions	Capacity to function	Financial system and devolution of funds		
1	2	3	4	5	6	7	8	9	10	11
1.	A	Kerala	2.0	1.5	2.0	3.0	15.0	3.0	26.5	85.48
2.	B	Gujarat*	1.5	1.0	1.0	0	5.0	1.0	9.5	30.64
3.		Haryana	2.0	1.0	1.0	0	4.5	1.5	10.0	32.25
4.		Karnataka***	1.0	1.0	1.0	0	5.0	1.0	9.0	29.03
5.		Maharashtra**	1.5	1.0	1.0	0	4.5	1.5	9.5	30.64
6.		Punjab*	1.5	1.0	1.0	0	4.5	1.5	9.5	30.64
7.		West Bengal	2.0	1.0	1.0	0	5.0	1.0	10.0	32.25
8.	C	Andhra Pradesh*	1.5	1.0	1.0	0	1.5	1.0	6.0	19.35
9.		Assam****	1.0	-	1.0	0	1.5	0	3.5	11.29

...(Contd.)

1	2	3	4	5	6	7	8	9	10	11
10.		Madhya Pradesh*	1.5	1.0	1.0	0	1.5	.5	5.5	17.24
11.		Meghalaya	NA	-	-	-	-	-	-	-
12.		Orissa	2.0	1.0	1.0	0	1.5	.5	6.0	19.35
13.		Rajasthan	2.0	1.0	1.0	0	1.5	.5	6.0	19.35
14.		Tamil Nadu	2.0	1.0	1.0	0	1.5	.5	6.0	19.35
15.		Uttar Pradesh	2.0	1.0	1.0	-2.0	1.5	.5	4.0	12.90

* Panchayat election delayed, and funds were not placed with ZPs till 1999.

** The term for the chairpersons reduced.

*** Panchayat elections delayed and the term for the chairpersons reduced.

**** Elections not held till 2000.

Note: The study of the above indicators is at the gram panchayat level, unless otherwise specifically mentioned.

SWOT Analysis of PR System

Strength

- **Constitutional status**
- **Scope for people's participation**
- Constitutional status and support
- Opportunities for the people to participation in the gram sabha for their village plan
- Well-defined structure
- Timely elections
- Representation for weaker sections
- Scope for devolution of financial power

Weaknesses

- **Low HRD level**
- **Poor capacity of PRIs**
- Lack of political will
- Lack of sufficient and trained manpower
- Lack of knowledge and skills in PR functionaries
- Lack of public awareness and vigilance, and lack of accountability
- Lack of funds at the panchayat level
- Decision-making in the hands of a few and failure to observe the rules
- Influence of elite group in the local development
- Lack of orientation of officials and staff for working with PRIs

Opportunity

- **Local knowledge in development**
- **Managing basic services**
- Utilization of local knowledge in the plan preparation
- Involvement of people in their village development planning
- Mobilization of resources in cash, kind or labour for local development
- Administration near to people for solving their problems
- Possibility of positive participation from poor and disadvantaged groups
- Increasing the sense of responsibility in people for managing their affairs

Threats

- **Dominance by a few**
- **Resistance by the existing government and traditional village set-up**
- Resistance at the state and national levels to share power
- Resistance from the rural elites and dominating class to share power with disadvantage groups
- Inadequate organizational support at GP and block levels for undertaking development works
- Low level of literacy and awareness among people
- Fear of concentration of power in a few hands
- The fear that traditional dominant classes may use the political and economic institutions (with legal sanctity) through their dominance to have their privileged position

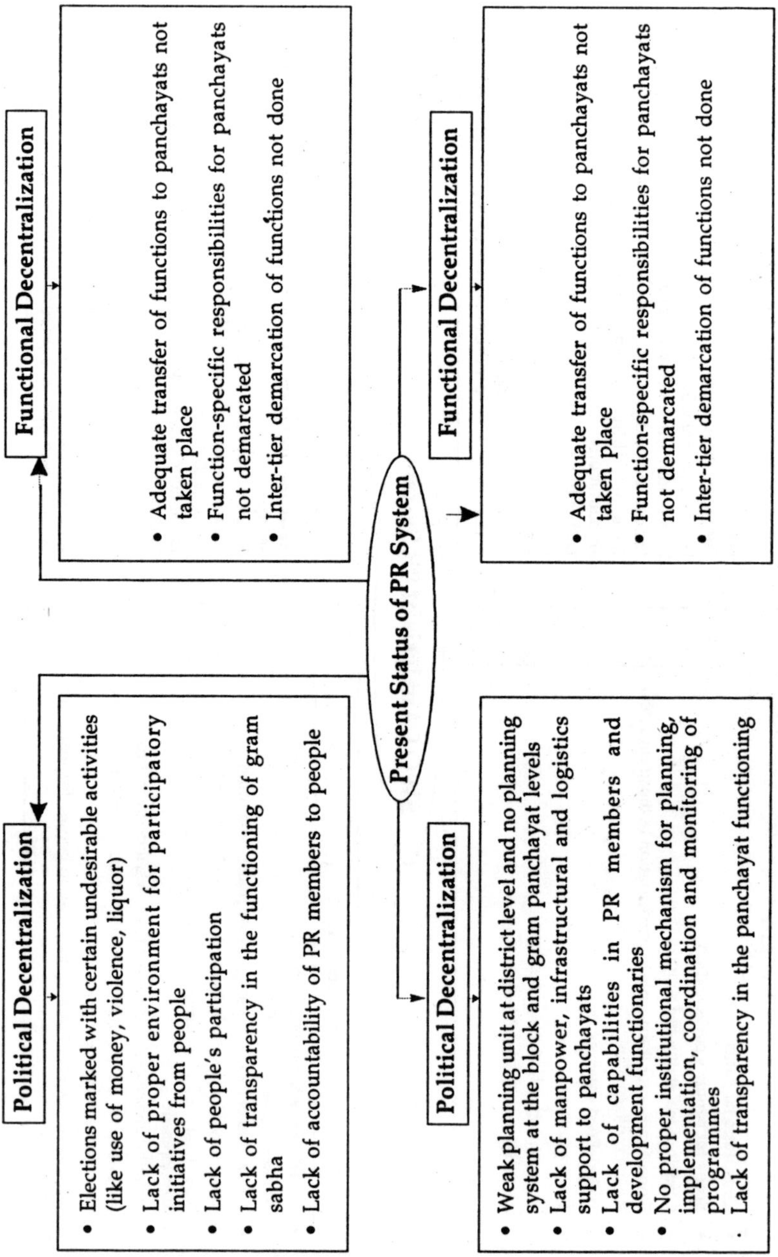

Fig. 3.5. Problems in the Present Form of PR System

unconducive for the individuals. In the villages, it does not encourage common people to get associated in the election process and to participate in the panchayat functioning in a meaningful way.

- If we look *from the point of people's participation,* it is still elusive. The studies are replete with instances (of shortcomings) when the people are not able to participate in the gram sabha. Besides, adequate efforts are not made by PR members to ensure their participation in the decision-making. Rather, the attempts are made to overlook their involvement. It is the chairperson of the gram panchayat or a few individuals who take the decisions. If we compare with the state of Kerala, it is evident in other states that the people's participation at the grassroots level is not forthcoming, and level of it is directly dependent on efforts made by the state government in this direction and the HRD level of people in the villages.
- When we look *from the point of planning,* no process or methodology has been formulated for the purpose of eliciting the information from people, database preparation, data analysis, and sectoral as well as backward-forward linkages analysis. In most of the cases, the selection of projects or the allocation of funds is done basically by the chairperson of the gram panchayat or by the members of his group. And no rational approach is followed while making panchayat plans.
- Also *from the point of implementation of programmes,* the beneficiaries involvement is almost absent. People are unaware about the cost of the project, the quantity of inputs used, number of people engaged, and so on. The execution and supervision of works remain the concern of chairperson of panchayat, or any agency or contractor identified by the panchayat.

- As far as *the point of transparency* is concerned, the information about the projects, beneficiaries' selection, inputs used in the projects, proceedings of the gram sabha and panchayat meetings are not within the reach of people.
- As regards *the point of responsiveness,* it has not been forthcoming from the PR members as people have to struggle hard to make their grievances heard. Similarly, issues of landless farmers, poor and weaker sections are not attended to by the panchayats in their action plan, nor are efforts made for evolving consensus in order to meet the problems of these target groups.
- If we examine *from the point of raising of own income* by the panchayats, the income is low, people are reluctant to paying taxes and the panchayats and the implementation of works.
- And *from the point of availability of services at the village level,* it is far from satisfactory, and people have to make rounds of visits to various offices for availing services.
- Finally, *from the point of accountability,* the chairpersons and the members of panchayats, in practice, are not accountable to people for their functional, administrative and financial decisions taken by them. Moreover, there is practically no sound mechanism or proper procedure for making them accountable for the actions taken by them.

Or in nutshell,

the fundamentals that are missing are:

- People's participation in discussion;
- Participatory planning;
- Responsiveness of PR members;
- Transparency in the panchayat functioning;
- Accountability of PR members;

inherent deficiencies are:

- Poor environment building;
- Poor HRD in the village; and

other vital deficiencies are:

- Wide socio-economic disparities
- Lack of focus on electoral reforms;
- Dominance of a few;
- Lack of focus on institution building; and
- Weak delivery system.

Thus, in the backdrop of above and the inferences drawn from the field studies, right from the planning, to implementation to supervision, to monitoring and to social audit, the people's participation is minimal. The chairpersons of panchayats or a few PR members and some influential individuals are the ones who take the decisions, and the people's involvement in the decision-making remains by and large absent. Not only this, there is a lack of transparency in the functioning of panchayats and the information is not made available to people. Even the decisions taken in the open gram sabha meeting are changed (especially the names of beneficiaries, which in some cases are pre-decided) while preparing the proceedings. Moreover, very little remedy is available to people for such a state of functioning of panchayats. PR members at all levels are more concerned with devolution of funds and control over officers and staff while important aspects like people's participation, transparency and accountability are completely overlooked.

In a way, the present system is not different from the previous development system (prior to 1993), in which the decision-making was centralized and the funds were allocated more by the choice of a few than by rational planning. The same mode of functioning has percolated from the then system to the present PR institutions. It is a pointer towards the unchecked drift of the philosophy of decentralization towards concentration of decision-making in a few hands. It has been mainly the result of the lack of attention given to important aspects in the operational terms. Though the gram sabha has been constituted in every village yet not much has been done to educate people about their rights and role in the village development. Similarly, transparency and accountability system has not got the desired place, and even if the panchayats or PR members do not perform as desired, people have very little control to ensure their propriety in the functioning. Also, institution building and the strengthening of delivery system are not the area, which get attention. Thus, the functioning of panchayats, continue without observing fundamentals. In this process the governance (especially in terms of accessing basic services) at the grassroot level remains a big casualty.

Thus, as reflected by the above discussion, in terms of fundamentals of decentralization, the present form of development system, even after the initiation of process of decentralization since 1993, is more or less an extension of previous system (the details are well–reflected by Table 3.19). It (system) is not able to meet basic needs of the people at the village level and that is leading to inadequacy of good governance. And, among others, the reassessment of various provisions enshrined in the amendment Act is very much needed.

Need for a Re-look at the Constitution Amendment Act

The analysis of various issues under different dimensions of decentralization has brought out that the panchayats at all the three tiers are not in a position to perform as expected. The pace and the direction of decentralization are not upto satisfactory level. Neither people are empowered to participate meaningfully, nor are their needs addressed, nor panchayats have the capacity to deliver as per the local needs, and nor are there organic linkages among the tiers. Even the Central Act is not able to address these vital issues, and moreover most of the provisions like on taxation, devolution

Table 3.19. How is the present Status of System of Decentralization vis-à-vis the Old System before 1992

S.No.	*From the point of view*	*Status prior to 1992 Act*	*Present status after 1992 Act*	*Remarks*
1	2	3	4	5
1.	Representation of people in the election	– Hold of traditional elites over panchayats – Disparities due to caste, class and gender influenced panchayats	– Village elites and political groups have more representation – Weaker sections and common person in the villages have little chance of getting true representation, due to hold of influential people and political parties	There is no perceptible difference in the quality of representation
2.	People's participation	– Participation of people in the development activities insignificant – Central decision-making	– The gram sabhas are dominated by only a few individuals – Poor and weaker sections do not have voice in the gram sabha	Participation of people remains poor and the decision-making is confined to a few people
3.	Planning	– By way of compilation of proposals from various departments – People were not involved adequately	– Compilation of proposals from various departments and people are not involved. No systematic planning procedure followed	No difference, same as before

1	2	3	4	5
4.	Implementation of works	– Implementation by the line departments, people not involved	– Works implemented by the chairpersons of panchayats – People do not take part in the implementation	Practically, no difference, same as before
5.	Supervision	– By the departments, people not involved	– By the chairperson and secretary of panchayat	No difference, same as before
6.	Availability of services at the village level	– Poor availability of services – Time consuming	– Poor availability of services – Time consuming	No difference, same as before
7.	Quality and efficiency	– Poor quality – Assets not properly utilized	– Poor quality of work – Marginal improvement in the implementation of work	In some cases marginal improvement in quality
8.	Level of generation of own income of panchayats	– Low income	– Low own income	No difference, same as before
9.	Responsiveness of functionaries at the decision-making level	– Lack of responsiveness of departments	– Lack of responsiveness of PR members	No difference, same as before
10.	Transparency	– Lack of transparency in the functioning of departments	– Lack of transparency in the panchayat functioning	No difference, same as before
11.	Accountability	– Lack of accountability of departments	– Lack of accountability of PR members to people	No difference, same as before

of funds and powers, etc. are indicative and not mandatory in nature. All these points towards for having a re-look at the 73rd Constitution Amendment Act, and for effecting necessary amendment in the backdrop of discussion presented in the preceding sections. The areas that require urgent attention are :

- Election of panchayat bodies;
- People's participation – role of gram sabha;
- Capacity of panchayats to function;
- Devolution of funds;
- Taxation;
- Constitution of various bodies such as DPC, SFC etc.;
- Organic linkages among tiers;
- Transparency;
- Accountability; and
- Arbitration

4
Demographic Profile of Sample States and Districts

CHHATTISGARH

History

The name Chhattisgarh is not ancient and has come into popular usage in the last few centuries. In ancient times, the region was called Dakshin Kosala. All inscription, literary works and the accounts of foreign travelers, call this region Kosala of Dakshin Kosala. According to Hari Thakur, the contest between Jabalpur and Chhattisgarh for the name of Mahakosala is settled beyond doubt in favour of Chhattisgarh in the light of available evidence. Even during the reign of Mughals, it was called Ratanpur territory and not Chhattisgarh. The word Chhattisgarh was popularized during the Maratha period and was first used in an official document in 1795.

A British Chronicler, J.B. Beglar provides the interesting story of explaining the origins of the name Chhattisgarh. It becomes very relevant in the context of contemporary caste consciousness and the caste configuration of the region. According to Beglas, "the real name of Chhattisghar and not Chhattisgarh. There is a tradition saying that ages ago about the time of Jarasandha, thirty six families of dalits (leather workers) emigrated southwards from Jarasandha's kingdom and established themselves in a country, which after them is called Chhattisgarh". Another common explanation regarding the origins of the name Chhattisgarh is that it denotes the number of forts in the region which are supposed to be thirty six in number. However, experts do not agree with this explanation, as thirty–six forts cannot be identified in the region. An explanation popular with the experts and historians is that Chhattisgarh is the corrupted from 'Chedisgarh' or the political seat of the Chedis.

According to mythological legend, Ram, during his *vanvas* stayed in Dakshin Kosala. Which is modern day Chhattisgarh. The unbroken history of Chhattisgarh or of South Kosala can be traced back to fourth century AD and its mythological history goes back as far as the *Mahabharata* and the *Ramayana*. About the history of the region, the famous historian C.W. Wills writes, 'in the 10th century AD a powerful Rajput family ruled at Tripuri near Jabalpur, issuing from this kingdom of Chedi (also known as Kalchuri dynasty) a scion of the royal house by the name Kalingraja, settled about the year 1000 AD, at Tuman, a site at present marked only by a few ruins in the north east of the erstwhile Laphazamindari of the Bilaspur district. His grandson Ratanraja founded Ratanpur which continued as the capital of a large part of the country now known as Chhattisgarh. This Rajput family called themselves the Haihaya dynasty. The dynasty continued ruling Chhattisgarh for six centuries about the 14th century it split into parts, the elder branch continued at Ratanpur, while the younger settled in semi–independent state at Raipur. At the end of 16th century, it acknowledged the suzerainty of the Mughals, in Bastar, in the middle ages, Chalukya dynasty established its rule. The first Chalukya ruler was Annmdev, who established the dynasty in Bastar in 1320.

The Marathas attacked Chhattisgarh in 1741 and destroyed the Haihaya power. In 1745 AD after conquering the region, they deposed Raghunathsinghji, the last surviving member of the Ratanpur house. In 1758, the Marathas finally annexed Chhattisgarh, it came directly under Maratha rule and Bimbaji Bhonsle was appointed the ruler. After the death of Bimbaji Bhonsle, the Marathas adopted the Suba system. The Maratha rule was a period of unrest and misrule. There was large scale loot and plunder by the Maratha army. The Maratha officials were openly surrendering the interests of the region to the British. As a result of this, the region became extremely poor and the people began resenting the Maratha rule. Only the Gonds continued to resist and challenge the advances of the Marathas and this led to several conflicts and much animosity between the Gonds and Marathas. The Pindaris also attacked and plundered the region in the beginning of the Nineteenth Century.

In 1818 Chhattisgarh came under some sort of British control for the first time. In 1854, when the province of Nagpur lapsed to the British government, Chhattisgarh was formed into a deputy commissionership with its headquarters at Raipur. Historian C.W. Wills, writing about Chhattisgarh says, Chhattisgarh presents the remarkable picture of a Hindu government continuing till modern times outside the sphere of direct Mohammedan control. The British made certain changes in the administrative and revenue system of Chhattisgarh, which adversely affected the people of Chhattisgarh. The intrusion of the British was resisted strongly in Bastar by the tribals and the Halba rebellion which lasted nearly five years (1774–1779) was the first documented rebellion against the British and Marathas in Bastar.

The first war of independence in 1857 was spearheaded in Chhattisgarh by Vir Narain Singh who was a benevolent jamindar of Sonakhan. The British arrested him in 1856 for looting a trader's grain stock and distributing it amongst the poor in severe famine years. In 1857, with the help of soldiers of the British Army at Raipur, Vir Narain Singh escaped from prison. He reached Sonakhan and formed an army of 500 men. Under the leadership of Smith, a powerful British army was dispatched to crush the Sonakhan army. The British succeeded after a prolonged battle and Vir Narain Singh was arrested and later hanged in the 10th of December 1857. He became the first martyr from Chhattisgarh in the War of Independence. Vir Narain Singh's martyrdom has resurrected in the 1980s and he has become a potent symbol of Chhattisgarhi pride.

The Movement for Prathak Chhattisgarh

The demand for a separate Chhattisgarh state was first raised in the early twenties. Similar demands kept cropping up at regular intervals; however, a well–organized movement was never launched. Several efforts were made by individuals and organizations towards highlighting the Chhattisgarh identity and expressing the sense of perceived marginalization. There were certain protests with mass support but these were limited and sporadic. There were several all-party platforms formed and they usually resolved around petitions, public meetings, seminars, rallies and bandhs.

A demand for separate Chhattisgarh was raised in 1924 by the Raipur Congress unit, and later on also discussed in the Annual session of the Indian Congress at Tripuri. A discussion also took place of forming a Regional Congress Organization for Chhattisgarh. Sporadic attempts to give a call for a separate state for Chhattisgarh continued in the years immediately following Independence. In 1955, a demand for a separate state was raised in the Nagpur assembly of the then state of Madhya Bharat.

When the State Reorganization Commission was set up in 1954, the demand for a separate Chhattisgarh was put forward to it, though this was not accepted. It was reported that the State Reorganization Commission rejected the demand for Chhattisgarh on the grounds that the prosperity of Chhattisgarh would compensate for the poverty of other regions of Madhya Pradesh.

The eighties were a comparatively quiet phase in the demand for Chhattisgarh. The 1990s saw more activity for a demand for the new state, such as formation of a state wide political forum, especially the Chhattisgarh Rajya Nirman Manch. The Late Chadulal Chandrakar led this forum, several successful region-wide Bandhs and rallies were organized under the banner of the forum all of which were supported by major political parties including the Congress and the BJP. The rallies of the all party forum were attended by leaders from most political parties.

Creation of Chhattisgarh

The Congress government of Madhya Pradesh took the first institutional and legislative initiative for the creation of Chhattisgarh. In the 18th of March 1994, a resolution demanding a separate Chhattisgarh was tabled and unanimously approved by the Madhya Pradesh Vidhan Sabha. Both the Congress and Bhartiya Janta Party supported the resolution. The election manifestos of the Congress and the BJP for both the 1998 and the 1999 Parliamentary elections as well as the Madhya Pradesh assembly election of 1998 included the demand for creation of separate Chhattisgarh. In 1998, the BJP led Union Government drafted a bill for the creation of a separate state of Chhattisgarh from sixteen districts of Madhya Pradesh. This draft bill was sent to the Madhya Pradesh Assembly for approval. It was unanimously approved in 1998, although with certain modifications. The union government did not survive and fresh elections were declared. The new National Democratic Alliance (NDA) government sent the redrafted Separate Chhattisgarh Bill for the approval of the Madhya Pradesh Assembly, where it was once again unanimously approved and then it was tabled in the Lok Sabha. This bill for a separate Chhattisgarh was passed in the Lok Sabha and the Rajya Sabha, paving the way for the creation of a separate state of Chhattisgarh. The President of India gave his consent to the Madhya Pradesh Reorganization Act 2000 on the 25th August 2000. The Government of India subsequently set the First day of November 2000 as the day on which the state of Madhya Pradesh would be bifurcated into Chhattisgarh and Madhya Pradesh. Many political observers have commented on the relatively peaceful manner in which the Chhattisgarh state has been created.

Location

Chhattisgarh is situated between 17 to 23.7 degree north latitudes and 8.40 to 83.38 east latitude. Chhattisgarh abounds with hilly regions and plains. It receives an annual rainfall of 60 inches. Uttar Pradesh to the north, Jharkhand to the north east, Orissa to the east, Andhra Pradesh to the south–east and south, Maharashtra to the south-west, Madhya Pradesh to the west and north west from its boundaries.

Area

The state of Chhattisgarh is spread over an area of 1,35,194 square kilometers.

Climate

The climate of Chhattisgarh is mainly tropical, humid and sub–humid. The climate is hot because of its positioning on the tropic of cancer. May is the hottest month and December – January are the coldest. The state is completely dependent on the monsoons for rains.

Physiography

The region has three divisions : Raipur, Bilaspur and Bastar. It is divided into three distinct land areas. In the north are Satpura ranges, in the centre are the plains of river Mahanadi and its tributaries and in the south is the plateau of Bastar. The total rainfall in the region is about 60 inches.

Chhattisgarh is rich in forest resources. About 44 per cent of the state is under forest cover. Chhattisgarh is famous in the entire country for its sal forests. In addition, teak, bamboo, saj, sarai, haldi etc., are also found in large numbers. Tendu leaf, which is used in *beeri* making is a principal forest produce of the state. Chhattisgarh produces a large number of minor forest products as well.

Soils

The region has yellow sandy soil that is suitable for the cultivation of rice.

Rivers

Mahanadi is the principal river of the state. Other major rivers are Sheonath, Hadeo, Mand, Eeb, Pairi, Jonk, Kelo, Udanti, Indrawati, Arpa and Maniyari.

Population

The total population of this newly created state, Chhattisgarh, as on 1st March 2001 stood at 20,795,956 as per the provisional results of the Census of India 2001. The population of the state rose by 18.06% during the decade 1991–2001, as against the national average of 21.34% during the same period.

The sex ratio (i.e. the number of females per thousand males) of population was recorded as 990, which has increased from 985 in the previous census. Total literacy of the state rose to 65.18% from 42.91% in 1991.

Table 4.1. Population Characteristics (2001)

Category	Number
Persons	20,795,956
Males	10,452,426
Females	10,343,530

Table 4.2. Decadal Growth 1991 – 2001

Category	*Percentage*
Persons	(+) 18.06
Males	(+) 17.81
Females	(+) 18.32

Table 4.3. Population (0 – 6 Years) (2001)

Category	*Number*
Persons	3,469,774
Males	1,756,441

Table 4.4. Percentage of Population (0–6 years) to Total Population (0 – 6 years) (2001)

Category	*Percentage*
Persons	16.68
Males	16.80
Females	16.56
Sex Ratio	975

Demographic Information

According to the 1991 census, the total population residing in the Chhattisgarh was 1.761 crores, which was 2.1 per cent of the population of India. The state of Chhattisgarh is carved out of 30.49 per cent of the land area and 26.6 per cent of the population of the undivided Madhya Pradesh, 95 cities and towns are in Chhattisgarh, including six class one towns.

Chhattisgarh has a population density of 130 persons per square km. The new state had an urbanization rate of 17.4 per cent in 1991, much lower than that of Madhya Pradesh, which was 25.3 per cent. Of the five main rajbhogi towns of undivided Madhya Pradesh, Chhattisgarh has one, Raipur.

The largest concentration of population for the state is in the districts in the central and north central parts. Raipur and Durg have the maximum population, which comprises 14.4

and 13.6 per cent of the states entire population in 1991. These two districts along with Bilaspur and Surguja make up for 47 per cent of the entire population. The spread of urban population also differs in its level of concentration.

Raipur and Durg account for almost half of the total urban population in Chhattisgarh. The other districts apart from Bilaspur and Rajanandgaon have less than six per cent urban population. The low urbanization is even more evident when we see that only four districts of Durg, Koriya, Raipur and Bilaspur had an urbanization rate of over 20 per cent in 1991.

As per 1991 census, the state of Chhattisgarh has 28.6 per cent of the total rural population of the undivided Madhya Pradesh. Chhattisgarh absorbs 37.1 per cent of the scheduled tribes and 22.3 per cent of the scheduled castes of the undivided Madhya Pradesh.

The gender ratio for Chhattisgarh according to the 1991 census was 985, which is very high when compared to most other regions of India. Except for Kerala, the new state of Chhattisgarh has a higher gender ratio than all other states. This does not include a comparison with the two other states of Uttaranchal and Vananchal.

The Infant mortality rate for the girl child in Chhattisgarh was 83 per 1000 live births in 1991. Looking at the overall trends in the IMR of undivided Madhya Pradesh, it has dropped from 119 for females in 1991 to 90 in 1997, and we can expect that the female IMR in Chhattisgarh would also have declined by around ten to fifteen percent.

The worker participation rate of 41 per cent for women in Chhattisgarh is much higher than the worker participation rate of 29.6 per cent for Madhya Pradesh. About 92 per cent of main workers amongst women were engaged in agriculture in 1991.

The state of Chhattisgarh came into being on 1 November 2000, when it was carved out of Madhya Pradesh. According to the 2001 census, the state has a total population of almost 2.1 crore. The state has 2,378 villages, 96 tehsils, 146 blocks and 16 districts. The first elections to the three levels of panchayats, after the formation of Chhattisgarh state, were held on January 2005.

Table 4.5. Name and Level of Three Tier Panchayat System

Level of Panchayat	*Name Used*
District Panchayat	Zila Panchayat
Intermediate Panchayat	Janpad Panchayat
Village Panchayat	Gram Panchayat

Table 3.6. Number of Panchayat Chairperson at Each Level

Sl. No.	*Name*	*Number*
1	Zila Panchayat	16
2	Janpad Panchayat	146
3	Gram Panchayat	9139
	Total	9301

Table 3.7. Number of Elected Panchayat Representatives at Each Level

	General	*SC*	*ST*	*Total*	*Women*
(A) Gram Panchayat					
Total no. of ward Member	71010	16336	60084	147430	49763
Total No. of Sarpanch	3448	864	5468	9820	3382
Grand Total of Elected Representatives	74498	17200	65552	157250	53045
Percentage	47.40	10.90	41.70	100.00	33.70
(B) Janpad Panchayat					
Total no. of Elected ward Members	1362	305	1164	2831	954
Percentage	48.10	10.80	41.10	100.00	33.70
(C) Zila Panchayat					
Total no. of Elected ward Members	153	35	117	305	103
Percentage	50.20	11.50	38.30	100.00	33.80

Source: Statistical Data of Chhattisgarh, 2006–07
Chattisgarh Panchayat Raj Adhiniyam

CHHATTISGARH

Raipur

The Chhattisgarh region has three divisions : Raipur, Bilaspur and Bastar. Raipur has a total population of 3,016,930 with the rural population being 2,099,312 and the urban population being 9,17,618. The males comprise 1,523,925 while the females are 1,493,005 in number. It is, the biggest city and has two Universities, one medical college, a radio station, television centre and an airport. Raipur has the only airport in the Chhattisgarh region. Khairagarh in Raipur division houses the famous Indira Sangeet Kala University. It also has the maximum population which comprises 14.4 per cent of the state's entire population in 1991. Raipur has less than 20 per cent Tribals, Scheduled Castes were over 15 per cent of the population in 1991. Also being, the state capital it is at the centre of the rail and road routes, between Mumbai and Kolkata, and is well connected to Delhi and Chennai. Raipur had an urbanization rate of over 20 per cent in 1991.

Bilaspur

Bilaspur has a total population of 1,998,355 persons with the rural population being 1,511,661 and the urban population being 486,694. Males comprise 1,013,875 of the population with females comprising 984,480 of the population. Its railway division is the most profitable railway operation in the country, contributing 17 per cent of the revenue of Indian Railways. Bilaspur had an urbanization rate of over 20 per cent in 1991.

UTTAR PRADESH

The history of Uttar Pradesh is very ancient and interesting. It is recognized in the later Vedic age as Brahmarshi Desha or Madhya Desha. Many great sages of the Vedic time like Bharadwaja, Gautam, Yagyavalkya, Vasishtha, Vishwamitra and Valmiki flourished in this state. Several sacred books of the Aryans were also composed here.

Two great epics of India, *Ramayana* and *Mahabharata*, appear to have been inspired by Uttar Pradesh.

In the sixth century BC, Uttar Pradesh was associated with two new religions – Jainism and Buddhism. It was at Sarnath that Buddha preached his first sermon and laid the foundations of his order and it was in Kushinagar in Uttar Pradesh where Buddha breathed his last. Several centres in Uttar Pradesh like Ayodhya, Prayag, Varanasi and Mathura became reputed centres of learning. In the medieval period, Uttar Pradesh was under Muslim rule and led the way to new synthesis of Hindu and Islamic cultures. Ramananda and his Muslim disciple Kabir, Tulsidas, Surdas and many other intellectuals contributed to the growth of Hindi and other languages.

Uttar Pradesh preserved its intellectual excellence even under the British administration. The British combined Agra and Oudh into the one province and called it United Provinces of Agra and Oudh. The name was shortened to the United Provinces in 1935. In January 1950, the United Provinces was renamed as Uttar Pradesh.

The earliest events which can safely be called historical are connected with the life of Gautam Buddha. The Sinhalese traditions place Gautam's death in 543 BC, while European scholars have suggested various dates between 477 and 370 BC. It is certain that he spent much of his life in the eastern districts, and the remains of Stupas, monasteries and other relics testify to the extent to which his doctrines were held in all parts of the Provinces as well as beyond their limits. A suggestion has recently been made that Buddhism was a regular development of religions. It among the people of Magadha and not merely a revolt against the growth of Brahmanism in Madhya Desha, as is commonly supposed. As a religious system, it appears to have maintained its position till the fourth century AD when a revival of Hinduism took place under the Guptas. The accounts of the Chinese pilgrims in the fifth and seventh century AD show that Buddhism was then fast waning, and the latest memorial of it as a living faith is an inscription of the twelfth or thirteenth century found in Gonda district.

The first point of contact with Western history comes in the fourth century BC, with Alexander's invasion and the subsequent relations of Seleucus Nicator with Sandrocottus, who is identified with Chandragupta Maurya of the Puranic annals. Chandragupta's kingdom, the first organized empire in India of which we have historical record, extended after the withdrawal of Seleucus, from the Hindu Kush to the Bay of Bengal, with its capital at Patna. The grandson of Chandragupta was Asoka, the first great Buddhist emperor, whose pious edicts have been found on pillars and rocks in many parts of India. Three of his inscriptions are known in these provinces, on pillars at Allahabad and Benares and on a rock at Kalsi in Dehradun. The last mentions by name of contemporary kings of Syria, Egypt, Macedonia, Cyrene and Epirus and thus fixes the date of Asoka's coronation at 270 or 269 BC. These inscriptions, and the fragments which have survived from writings of Megasthenese, the ambassador of Seleucus at the court of Patna, show a highly developed system of government.

If the chronology of the Puranas is to be accepted, the Mauryan dynasty came to an end about 188 or 178 BC, and was succeeded by the Sunga, but there is no independent confirmation of this. Numismatic evidence points to the conclusion that parts of at least four kingdoms were included in the provinces, corresponding to the ancient Surasena (round Mathura), North Panchala (Rohilkhand), Kosala (round Ayodhya), and a tract south of Allahabad which may have been the kingdom of Kosambhi during this time. From their coins the kings of Panchala and Mathura appear to have been Hindus, while the symbols on the coins of Ayodhya and Kosambhi are often Buddhist.

The Provinces had been free from foreign invaders for about four hundred years, when in 1018, Mahmud of Ghazni crossed the Yamuna, and took Bulandshahr, the rich city of Mathura with its temples full of jewels and gold, and Kannauj. This expedition and two more in 1021 and 1023 directed against Kannauj, Gwalior and Kalingar were mere raids, in which plunder rather than conquest was the aim.

Early in the sixteenth century the capital was moved from Delhi to Agra, which was to become a great city under the Mongols or Mughals, who now appeared again. In 1526, Babar defeated the Afghàn king, Ibrahim at Panipat but found himself in difficulties at Agra. On the west, the Rajputs were united under the Rana of Udaipur, while on the east, the Afghans were threatening an attack from Kannauj. The crown prince, Humayun made a successful raid as far as Jaunpur and Ghazipur and Babar gained a great victory over the Rajputs near Fatehpur Sikri.

After the death of Akbar in 1605 at Agra, his son succeeded as Jahangir. In 1623 Khurram, another son of the emperor, rebelled and advanced towards Mathura, but was driven back to Central India. On Jahangir's death at Lahore in 1627, Khurram hastened to Agra and obtained the throne under the name of Shah Jahan. Early in his reign the Bundelas, who had been turbulent throughout Akbar's life, but had been friendly to Jahangir broke out and several expeditions were sent against them. Aurangzeb entered Agra in 1658 and he formally assumed the throne at Lahore.

After the death of Aurangzeb in 1707, he left a will advising his three sons to divide the empire. The second son, Azam refused to accept the division and fell in battle at Jajau in Agra, fighting the eldest brother Muazzam, who became the emperor under the title of Shah Alam Bahadur.

At the commencement of the nineteenth century, the British thus held only the present Benares division (except South Mirzapur) and the fort of Allahabad. In 1801, when Rohilkhand and other parts of the Oudh territory were in a state of anarchy, and a grandson of Ahmad Shah Durrani was threatening to invade India, Saadat Ali, Nawab of Oudh, in return for a guarantee of protection, made over to the British the so–called 'Ceded Provinces', which included the present Gorakhpur and Rohilkhand divisions, with the districts of Allahabad, Fatehpur, Kanpur, Etawah, Mainpuri, Etah, the south of Mirzapur, and the Tarai parganas of the Kumaun division.

The early Muhammadens have left many memorials in the shape of mosques, idgahs and tombs. The oldest among these are some buildings constructed at Budaun by the emperor Altamsh in the beginning of the thirteenth century. The finest specimens are, however, the great mosques at Jaunpur, built two hundred years later by the Sharki kings, which are particularly striking for their huge facades, recalling the propylons of Egypt.

During the sixteenth and seventeenth centuries, the emperors Akbar, Jahangir, and Shah Jahan spent large sums on the adornment of the royal residences at Fatehpur Sikri and Agra, where stately palaces, magnificent tombs and mosques still recall the memories of the great Mughals. Much has been done within the last few years to repair and preserve these valuable monuments. In the eighteenth century, the type of architecture deteriorated, though buildings of some beauty were built by the Rohillas and the early Nawabs of Oudh.

Location

Uttar Pradesh is truly the heart land of India situated in Northern India and shares its border with Himachal, Punjab, Delhi, Madhya Pradesh, Bihar and international border with Nepal. It lies between latitude of 24 degrees to 31 degrees and longitude of 77 degree to 54 degrees.

Area

Uttar Pradesh has an area of 2.94 million square kilometer. Area wise it is fourth largest state.

Physiography

Uttar Pradesh can be divided into three distinct regions :

- The Himalayan region in the north
- The Gangetic plain in the centre
- The Vindhya hills and Plateau in the south.

The transitional belt running along the entire length of the state is called the *terai* and *bhabhar* areas. The main crops are wheat, rice and sugarcane.

The Gangetic plain is watered by the Yamuna, the Ganga and its major tributaries, the Ram Ganga, the Gomti, the Ghaghra and Gandak. The whole plain is alluvial and very fertile. The chief crops cultivated here are rice, wheat, millets, gram, barley. Sugar cane is the chief cash crop of the region. The southern fringe of the Gangetic plain is demarcated by the Vindhya hills and plateau. It has four distinct kinds of soil, two of which are agriculturally difficult to manage. They are black cotton soil.

Rainfall is scanty and erratic and water resources are scarce. Dry farming is practiced on a large scale.

Climate

The climate of the state is tropically monsoon, but variations exist because of difference in altitudes. The Himalayan region is cold. The average temperature varies in the plains from 3 to 4°C in January to 43 – 45°C in May and June. There are three distinct seasons – the winter season from October to February, summer from March to mid–June and the rainy season from June to September. The Himalayan region has about 100–200 cm. of rainfall.

Floods are a recurring problem of the states causing damage to crops, life and property. There are occasional cloud bursts adding to the misery of the people. The proneness is ascribed to the heavy rainfall, low flat country, high sub-soil, water level and the silting of beds which causes river levels to rise. Poor drainage is caused by obstruction of roads, railways, canals, new built–up areas.

Soil

The valley area has fertile and rich soil. There is an intensive cultivation on terraced hill slopes. The higher altitudes are suitable for sub–tropical and temperate fruit culture. The Siwalik range, which forms the southern foot hills of the Himalayas, slopes down into a boulder bed called 'bhadhar'.

Hills

The prominent peaks in the hill region include Banarpunch, Mount Kamety, Trishul, Dunagiri, Nanda Devi, Badrinath and Kedarnath. The hill areas are sparsely populated. Due to the excessive nature of the terrain, soil is subject to heavy erosion. Cultivation is done under intensive soil. Irrigation facilities are deficient and only a small fraction of the total area is under artificial irrigation.

Rivers

The major rivers are the Ganga, Yamuna, Gomti, Ghaghra, Rapti, Sarda and Ramganga.

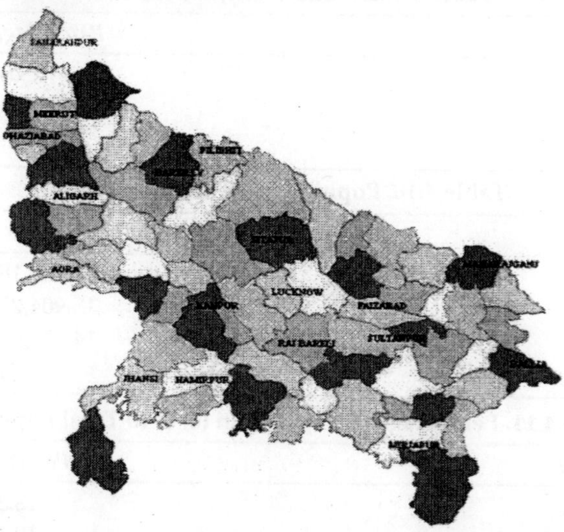

POLITICAL MAP OF UTTAR PRADESH

Population of Uttar Pradesh

Despite carving out a separate state of Uttaranchal from Uttar Pradesh, the state is still way ahead of all states and Union territories in terms of population. Its population as on 1st March 2001 stood at 166,052,859 as per the provisional results of the Census of India 2001.

The population of the state rose by 25.80 per cent during the decade 1991–2001. The sex ratio (i.e. the number of females per thousand males) of population is recorded as 898, which has improved from 876 worked out during the previous census. Total literacy of the state rose to 57.36 per cent from 40.71 per cent in 1991.

Table 4.8. Population 2001

Category	*Number*
Persons	166,052,859
Males	87,466,301
Females	78,586,558
Sex Ratio	898

Table 4.9. Decadal Growth 1991– 2001

Category	*Percentage*
Persons	(+) 25.80
Males	(+) 24.31
Females	(+) 27.50

Table 4.10. Population (0 – 6 Years), 2001

Category	*Number*
Persons	30,459,187
Males	15,904,256
Females	14,554,931
Sex Ratio	916

Table 4.11. Percentage of Population (0–6) to Total Population

Category	*Percentage*
Persons	18.35
Males	18.18
Females	18.54

The central fact of the social order in Uttar Pradesh is the existence of the caste system among the Hindus who constitute the vast majority of the population.

A separate sub–caste, which is lower than the full blooded Brahmins in hierarchy but higher than the Kshatriyas, thereby came into existence, known as Bhumihars. Several others like Khatris and Bishnois can be cited. These arose out of an intermixture of blood and other factors.

The rigid caste attitude in the past and the social and political tensions have resulted in the growth of large settlements of particular castes in compact regions in Uttar Pradesh. Thus, there are large pockets of Ahirs, Gujars, Kurmis, Bhumihars, and so on in different parts. The Scheduled Castes and the Harijans have their own settlements everywhere. The village leadership is in the hands of upper castes while in the urban areas, the trading class (Vaishyas) with plenty of money to spend, is a well–knit community and has a large say in direction of affairs.

The Muslims are not evenly distributed over the state. They are found in western division of Meerut, Agra and Rohilkhand and in the eastern districts in Terai area in Gonda and Baharaich, in Azamgarh, Jaunpur and Ghazipur.

The fertile plains of Uttar Pradesh offered an ideal habitat for the early Muslim settlers who came in the wake of the establishment of Turkish rule in India. The hostility was confined mainly within the ruling classes – The Rajas, Rawats, Rais and the original village echelons and the muqtis and their subordinates. Years before the Ghurid conquest of northern India, the Muslims had settled in Badaun, Bahraich, Kannauj, Unnao and Bilgram. Muslim concentration in towns was primarily due to their socio–political organizations, their exclusive racial and religious complexion. Muslims have always had an influential upper class consisting of Nawabs, Rajas and Chaudhries because of their historical antecedents.

The middle class, comparatively thin among Muslims, is engaged in the traditional trades like leather, timber (in the terai area), tobacco and perfume (in Lucknow). There is only a sprinkling of Muslims in the services and professions. Commerce and trade was not a Muslim forte.

A part of Uttar Pradesh mainly tribal areas with the following districts such as Dehradun, Uttarkashi, Tehri Garhwal, Rudraprayag, Chamoli, Hardwar, Pauri Garhwal, Bageshwar, Pithoragarh, Almora, Nainital, Champawat and Udham Singh Nagar has been formed into a new state Uttaranchal. So part of the tribal population is now in the state of Uttaranchal.

The population of the tribal communities in the state is not large. They constitute the weakest section of the society and form distinct ethnic groups which have preserved their own separate culture identities in their original environment despite the ravages of time.

Uttar Pradesh's greatest gifts to humanity are the two epics, *'Ramayana'* and *'Mahabharata'*. From the epic age, the territory of Uttar Pradesh is being watered by several fresh streams of culture, the two most significant being those generated by the teachings of the Buddha and Mahavira, the 24th Jain Tirthankar.

UTTAR PRADESH : SAMPLED DISTRICTS

Gonda

The district Gonda is situated in U.P. with tehsils, Gonda, Colonelganj, Tarabganj, Mankapur and Paraspur. Its area in square kilometers is 3788 kms., with a population of 27,65,586 as per 2001 census, with the rural population being 2,51,267 and the urban population being 194,319. The gender ratio was nearly equal, males comprising 1,451,101 and females being 1,314,485. There is a large dam in Gonda named Khairman, its year of completion being 1958. There are a number of fairs and festivals held in Gonda namely Bijleshwari Devi fair which is held in Balrampur in the month of Ashadha (June–July). It is attended by thousands of persons every year. Another fair is Chhap a Jatra which is held 50 kms. from Gonda. Then there is Devi Patan fair which is held in Tulsipur near Gonda from 1st to 15th of first half of Chaitra (March–April). There is a big daily newspaper named *Mother*, its language being Hindi. Its place of publication is Gonda with a circulation of 77,150.

Sitapur

The district Sitapur is situated in U.P. with tehsils Misrikh, Sitapur, Laharpur, Biswan, Mahmudabad and Sidhauli. Its area in square kilometers is 5743 km. with a total population of 3,619,661 as per 2001 census, with the rural population being 3,186,973 and the urban population being 432,688. Males comprise 1,941,374 of the population while females are 1,678,287 in number. There are a number of fairs and festivals held in Sitapur namely Dhanush Yajna fair which is held on Hargaon in Sitapur area for about a week in the month of Karthik (October–November) and ends on the day of full moon. Then there is Naimisharanya Jatra which is a bathing fair. Then there is Nauchandi fair which is held in March or beginning of April. There is a medium daily newspaper titled *Vyas Bharti*, its language being Hindi, its place of publication being Sitapur with a circulation of 27342 (2001).

Panchayati Raj in Uttar Pradesh

The scheme of Panchayati Raj was an effort to provide for an integrated system of local government in the rural areas, with functions of development necessitated by the governmental functions. Planning and development became the *sine qua non* of the rearrangement of its structure and functions.

When Mehta Committee's recommendations came up for discussion, adoption and implementation, U.P. did not quite approve of the three tier structure. The Minister of Local Self–Government, Sri Vichitra Narain Sharma, maintained during the Third Meeting of the Central Council of Local Self–Government in September, 1957, that "in my state there will be nearly 366 blocks. But .... I do not think I will be able to guide them and really give them that kind of education which they require. We shall perforce have to involve another agency between the state and these blocks, because these blocks will be too big and we will not be able to get sufficient good personnel to correctly guide and administer these units.... We are thinking that the District Boards should be made more effective. It should be given greatest powers. The work of planning must be entrusted to the district boards. In fact, many other things which we are doing today at the state level may be perhaps safely handed over to them.

Thus, U.P. favoured further strengthening of the district rather than making the intermediary institution (at the Block) the real agency for planning. Thus, under the Antarim Zila Parishad Act, the emphasis was on the district. The first bill to introduce statutory Zila Parishads, was discussed at the Fourth Meeting of the Central Council of Local Self–Government in October 1958 which suggested major changes. The bill was redrafted and introduced in the U.P. Legislature in August 1959. The Uttar Pradesh Kshetra Samitis and Zila Parishads Adhiniyam was finally passed on May 19, 1961 and received the President's assent on November 22, 1961. The purpose of the Adhiniyam is stated thus : " ... it is expedient to provide for the establishment of Kshetra Samitis and Zila Parishads in the districts of Uttar Pradesh to undertake certain governmental functions at Kshetra and district levels respectively in furtherance of the principle of democratic decentralization of governmental functions and of ensuring proper municipal government in rural areas, and to correlate the powers under Uttar Pradesh Provinces Panchayat Raj Act 1947, with Kshetra Samitis and Zila Parishads ...".

Thus, the structure was built up from the already existing Gram Panchayats, established under the Act of 1947. Under the new Act of 1961, arrangements were made to connect these Panchayats with institutions situated at the block and district levels.

Development of rural self–government has followed a pattern of expansion in coverage as well as functions. They started as purely governmental institutions, consisting only of nominated members and performing municipal functions. Slowly the base of 'legitimacy' of these institutions improved with enlarging electorates. Expansion of functions was, however, slower. Establishment of Panchayati Raj on the basis of U.P. Zila Parishad and Kshetra Samitis Adhiniyam of 1961, marks the culmination of this process of evolution. The Village Panchayats, constituted by adult franchise, provides the base for this structure with formal institutional integration at successively higher levels i.e., the Block and District levels. The long list of all inclusive development functions seem to overshadow the traditional municipal functions.

Tiered structure of rural Local Self–Government with integrated membership has been suggested by various Commissions and Committees and has been tried in U.P. even before Balvant Mehta Scheme was introduced. Lord Ripon's Resolution of 1882 suggested for the setting up of Local Boards at sub–division, or taluka or tehsil levels and also district board. The implementing Act of 1883 set up Local Board (at tehsil level) and District Boards. District Board members coming from a particular tehsil became members of Local Boards of the area. These Local Boards, however, did not find a place in District Boards Act of 1906. A scheme of the election of District Board members by the members of Village Panchayats was suggested by the Decentralization Commission Report of 1909. The Local Self-Government Committee Report of 1938 suggested for a three-tier structure of Village Panchayats, Pargana Committees and District Boards.

What was new in the Mehta scheme was that the intermediary level was the developmental unit i.e., the Community Development Block, rather than the revenue unit of sub–division or taluka or tehsil. This necessity, to be sure arose out of the enlarged functions of these institutions as also the situational existence of the blocks. Thus, the Mehta scheme was a result of an effort to combine the past experience of the working of local bodies and the new functions of development : "It is argued that as there was not enough responsibility entrusted to the local bodies, they did not offer any challenge to the initiative of leadership, and therefore, became prey to public apathy. The failure of Community Development Programme was attributed to the inability of government officers to involve local leaders in major decision regarding development. The Study Team on Community Projects combined these arguments to advocate a total reorganization of local bodies as well as the Community Development Programme".

As the objective of the U.P. Kshetra Samitis and Zila Parishads Adhiniyam 1961 declares, the purpose was to formalize the existing institutions at the village, district and the block into an integrated Panchayati Raj set up.

Tiered structure of local government originating at the Village Panchayat, and integration at successively higher levels, was almost an ideological commitment with the Congress Party during the Independence struggle. The outline is provided in the Gandhian constitution for Green India, advocating for an elected Village Panchayat as the base and upward integration to talukas, district, province and finally to the central level. The scheme was debated at length in the Constituent Assembly and was finally referred to the Constitutional Advisor. This arrangement of institutions did not find favour on purely tactical grounds that its adoption would mean a complete revision of the Constitution, which was at the final draft stage.

The continued existence of the Congress party was the most important factor which facilitated the panchayat movement. However, a significant and interesting point mentioned by the advocates of Village Panchayat was that since the panchayat was an institution with which the Indian village population was familiar, its provision will provide legitimacy to the Constitution, specially when 'there is nothing Indian in the Constitution".

As regards the powers and functions, it clearly suggests their revolving nature over a period of time. The functions of the Zila Parishad and the Village Panchayats are not much different from the District Boards and the Panchayats.It is the Kshetra Samiti which has got powers and duties that may be called new. The shadow of the Community Development Programme over the Kshetra Samiti is clear not only from the functions but also the staffing pattern and the finances. The units of the Panchayati Raj organization are treated as purely administrative, owing their existence and geographical coverage to the convenience of the State Government : a re-delimitation of the Community Development Blocks introduced in July 1966 abolished 198 Blocks in 45 district in U.P. The Village Panchayats within these Kshetra Samitis were apportioned to the adjoining areas. Membership of the Zila Parishads also had to be adjusted. These political units were organized on the basis of legislative authorization and having directly elected membership, were changed as a result of administrative fiat.

The structure of Panchayati Raj does not represent any break from the past institutions or proposals of local government. The set up introduced by the Mehta Committee Report, is a result of the evolutionary process outlined above. The Panchayati Raj Institutions are functioning under the constraints of the 'legacies' of the myth of ancient village 'little republics', the pre-Independence commitments of the Congress party and a purely government sponsored Community Development Programme.

Uttar Pradesh brought in Panchayati Raj immediately after independence through the enactment of the U.P. Panchayat Act, 1947. Following the recommendations of the Balwant Rai Mehta Committee, a three-tier system of Panchayats was established through the enactment of the U.P. Kshetra Samitis and Zila Parishad Act of 1961 (termed as U.P. Kshetra Panchayat and Zila Panchayat Adhiniyam, 1961).

Table 4.12. Nomenclature of Three Levels of Panchayats

Level of Panchayat	*Name Used*
District Panchayat	Zila Panchayat
Intermediate Panchayat	Kshetra Panchayat
Village Panchayat	Gram Panchayat

Reservation of Women

(a)	Pradhan of Gram Panchayat	50%
(b)	Member of Gram Panchayat	38%
(c)	Pramukh of Kshetra Panchayat	51%
(d)	Member of Kshetra Panchayat	37%
(e)	Adhyaksha of Zila Panchayat	76%
(f)	Member of Zila Panchayat	40%

Panchayat	*General*	*SC*	*ST*	*Total*	*Women*
Gram Panchayat	527779	174842	673	703294	273229
Percentage	75.04	24.86	0.10		38.85
Kshetra Panchayat	49164	16453	52	65669	24674
Percentage	74.87	25.05	0.08	100.00	37.5
Zila Panchayat	2041	655	2	2698	1122
Percentage	75.65	24.28	0.07	100.00	41.59

Source: State Government of U.P.

Women Empowerment Schemes in Chhattisgarh

1. Indira Sahara Yojana

This is under the State Social Security Scheme.

- Coverage @ Rs. 150/– of all destitute persons above 60 years or more and destitute persons with disability above 14 years.
- National Old Age Pension Scheme
- Started from 2nd October 1995, covers all destitute persons above 65 years of age, with assistance @ Rs. 75 from Government of India and @ Rs. 75 from State Government.

- Scheme Outline : Indira Sahara Yojana launched on 19th November 2000 ahead of women empowerment year 2001–02.
- Social security Cover extended to age group 18–50, under Indira Sahara.
- Social Security Assistance is Rs. 150 per month.
- Identification by Gram Sabha in Rural Areas.
- Assistance sanctioned by Gram Panchayats and urban Local Bodies.
- Eligibility for benefits : widow/ divorcee/ destitute/ disability with no means of income and nor any one to look after.
- Payment made in Gram Sabhas are at the General meeting of Gram Panchayats.
- Beneficiaries encouraged to form self–help groups.
- Training and skill formation imparted to those joining self–help groups.

2. Indira Soochna Shakti Scheme

Objectives

(i) Computer education and access to information technology for girl students.

(ii) Creating environment for e–governance.

(iii) Opening up of possibility of distance learning and networking.

(iv) Promoting community/ NGO/ Private sector involvement.

Features

(i) For girl students.

(ii) Covers classes 9, 10, 11 and 12

(iii) Started in Co–education schools/ High schools and Higher Secondary Schools managed by Panchayati Raj Institutions/ Urban Local Bodies.

(iv) Largest IT education scheme for girls at secondary level in India.

(v) Free enrolment for girls from SC/ ST families and from BPL families, belonging to OBC and other categories.

(vi) Free for girl students in eligible schools.

(vii) 100 hours of IT education on CBSE syllabus spread upto 10 months of academic year.

(viii) Opportunity to boys only schools to avail IT education on payment of nominal fees.

(ix) At least 5 Pentium Computers with Internet per school with one IT instructor per batch of 20 students.

(x) Example of Public–private partnership.

(xi) Girl trained under this will manage similar institutions voluntarily in projects.

Implementation–Meetings

(a) Policy Level –chaired by CM

(b) Official Level – Secretary, School Education and other officials.

Funding

(i) Being funded from State Budget,

(ii) Current year's outlay – Rs. 7 crores

(iii) Government of India and Departments of Tribal Affairs and Women and Child Development for financial assistance.

(iv) With increasing number of students, competitor would drive the fee structure down in future.

Constraints

(i) Internet connectivity not available.

(ii) Lack of rooms and electricity in villages.

3. Indira Mahila Kosh

- Women in Chhattisgarh have a comparatively higher status within families and in society.

- Chhattisgarh gender ratio of 990 women to 1000 men is third after Kerala and Pondicherry.
- Women constitute 36.5 per cent of working population.
- Kosh – initial corpus of Rs.1 crore.
- Governing body is headed by Minister for Women and Child Development.

Functions

(i) Promoting women empowerment.

(ii) Providing financial assistance for sustaining current occupation and employment.

(iii) Encouraging investment and creating income generation opportunities.

(iv) Creating productive assets.

(v) Capital formation

(vi) Meeting contingent credit requirements.

4. Self–Help Groups in Chhattisgarh

Functions

(i) Organizing SHGs among women beneficiaries.

(ii) Equipping weaker sections of women through innovation scheme.

(iii) Sensitizing administrative setups and delivery mechanism towards co–option of women and their developmental process participation.

(iv) Commissioning research projects on socio–economic issues pertaining to women.

(v) Networking women groups. NGOs and other resources.

(vi) Entrepreneurship development.

(vii) Accessing and catalyzing other financial institutions, Central and State Government.

(viii) Mobilizing resources from other quarters.

(ix) Assistance in project design and formulation.

(x) Providing opportunities and forum for exchange of ideas and information relevant to empowerment of women.

Women Empowerment

Women empowerment is mainly concerned with providing women with a platform towards achieving economic as well as social independence. It focuses on equal sharing of resources and opportunities between men and women. The measures to achieve this would be changes in women's mobility in the social ladder, changes in women labour patterns, and changes in women's access to control over resources. This can be done through education, welfare schemes and policy measures. Education means equality – social, legal, economic, educational and political. Structural and attitudinal changes across sections are necessary. Socio–economic status of women should be raised.

Social evils such as female foeticide and gender bias should be curbed. There is a low female literacy rate, 40 per cent (1991). This is accompanied by a high drop out rate of girls in schools. There are backward cultural ideologies and religious values, caste system, sexism, religion, regional differences and rural urban disparities.

Strategies for Women Empowerment

1. Awareness generation initiatives
2. Self–employment through credit and training
3. Lean season wage employment
4. Saving habit
5. Range of support services
6. Minimum needs satisfaction, such as nutrition, sanitation, housing and education
7. Direct involvement of women in development programmes.
8. Poverty reduction.

Requirement of Women Entrepreneurs

1. Courage and self–confidence
2. Sharing of time in family and business activities
3. Learning new things and training
4. Change from production orientation to marketing oriented
5. Effective decision making and risk taking
6. Acceptance to change
7. Elimination of unnecessary activities
8. Good relationship and working atmosphere.

Problems of Women Entrepreneurs

1. Financial constraints
2. Stiff competition
3. Inefficient arrangement
4. Over dependence on intermediaries
5. Scarcity of raw materials
6. Social status
7. Lack of education
8. High cost of production
9. Low mobility
10. Family responsibility
11. Low ability to bear risk
12. Low need for achievement
13. Absence of ambition for achievement

Remedies

1. Finance cells to marketing cooperatives
2. Supply of raw material
3. Education and awareness
4. Training facilities

Components of Effective Training Programme for Indian Women are

1. Career
2. Attitudinal change
3. Assertiveness training
4. Project formulation and implementation
5. Post training support and following services like promotional meetings, advertisements and publicity
6. Professional management skill
7. Effective communication skill and practice
8. Assuming responsibility
9. Increase of knowledge.

Steps in Entrepreneurial Process

1. Decision to be self-employed
2. Selection of product
3. Registration
4. Statutory license clearance
5. Procurement of machinery
6. Recruitment of personnel
7. Power connection/ water supply
8. Production
9. Repayment of loans
10. Avoiding sickness
11. Location of enterprise
12. Preparation of project report
13. Finance (Term loan)
14. Land and building
15. Installation of machinery
16. Procurement of raw material

17. Marketing
18. Profit generation
19. Modernization and upgradation of technology.

Functions and Role of Women Entrepreneurs

1. Explore prospects of starting new enterprise
2. Uncertainty of risk and handling of economic uncertainties
3. Coordination, administration and control
4. Routine supervision.

Types of Industrial Enterprises Suitable for Women Entrepreneurs

1. Operate purely as a sub–contractor on raw material provided by customer
2. Manufacture an item to the large scale unit
3. Manufacture item for direct sale in the market

The socio-economic characteristics of women representatives are not different from any other women in Indian society. Most of the women who stood for the elections and won were in the age group of 35–55 years. Less than one fourth of the women, compared to three fourth of men, had previous political experience. Most of the women were from the dominating caste, however, reservation for downtrodden castes added a margin of representation for these groups. Less than five percent of women as against twenty percent of men were found professionally educated. The majority of women representatives were engaged in domestic work, household activities including agriculture operation and other unorganized economic activities. They lack resources and need capacity building. Most of the elected women representatives are not aware about their duties as panchayat functionaries. Thus, the effective functioning of Panchayats could not be ensured. Caste polarization is prevalent and Panchayats and women representatives work with their own caste group. They depend heavily on their husbands and in laws to resolve the problems presented to them. Women representatives at the higher tiers are often more educated and experienced and therefore, they are more vocal and participative in meetings as compared to women members in gram panchayat meetings. Women's participation in constituted committees is negligible and male members dominate such committees. Male members attempt to dominate the meeting without giving any space to women members to participate. Women members also lack confidence while women from dominating castes are more vocal in meetings. Social customs and values also prevent women to speak before men. Physical violence in panchayat elections and meetings often impedes women's participation in Panchayati Raj. Government offices are also indifferent towards women representatives but they respond immediately to male representatives. It is rightly observed that women representatives are for name sake, the real power lies with husbands, or male members of the household.

Women's Representation in Panchayats in U.P.

Women representation in the first election in 1995, after the new Panchayati Raj System in Uttar Pradesh (including Uttaranchal) was reported 33 per cent and 33.32 per cent respectively against total number of pradhans and members at Gram Panchayats. Similarly at block level Panchayats 33.29 per cent and 33.32 per cent women were elected as Pramukh and member while at the district level, panchayat women constituted 34.96 and 32.37 per cent respectively as Adhyaksha and member.

The second elections held in 2000 for rural local bodies (excluding Uttaranchal) demonstrated much higher share of women representation as against the one third reserved seats. On comparing statistics of the two elections, it is found that there has been increase of 4.69 per cent in representation of women at district level panchayat members and 4.63 per cent in gram panchayat members. Again at Kshetra Panchayat

Table 4.13. Women Representation in Panchayats in U.P. (1995) (Including Uttaranchal State)

Particulars	*Gram Panchayats*		*Kshetra Panchayats*		*Zila Panchayats*	
	Pradhan	*Member*	*Pramukh*	*Member*	*Adhyksh*	*Member*
Total	58620 (100.0)	673601 (100.0)	904 (100.0)	57288 (100.0)	83 (100.0)	2528 (100.0)
ST	117 (0.20)	1347 (0.20)	2 (0.22)	114 (0.20)	— —	5 (0.19)
Male	78 (0.13)	898 (0.13)	1 (0.11)	76 (0.13)	—	4 (0.16)
Female	39 (0.07)	449 (0.00)	1 (0.11)	38 (0.07)	—	1 (0.04)
SC	12341 (21.05)	141456 (20.94)	189 (20.91)	12030 (20.99)	18 (21.68)	531 (21.00)
Male	8269 (14.11)	94304 (13.99)	126 (13.94)	8020 (13.99)	11 (13.25)	354 (14.00)
Female	4072 (6.95)	47152 (6.99)	63 (6.97)	4010 (6.99)	7 (8.43)	177 (7.00)
OBC	15827 (26.99)	181872 (26.99)	243 (26.88)	15469 (27.00)	25 (30.12)	683 (27.02)
Male	10604 (18.09)	121248 (17.99)	162 (17.92)	10313 (18.00)	17 (20.48)	456 (18.04)
Female	5223 (8.90)	60624 (8.99)	81 (8.96)	5150 (9.00)	8 (9.64)	227 (8.08)
Unreserved	30335 (51.75)	3248926 (51.80)	470 (51.99)	29675 (51.80)	40 (48.19)	1309 (51.78)
Male	20324 (34.67)	232618 (34.53)	314 (34.73)	19784 (34.53)	26 (31.32)	873 (34.53)
Female	10011 (17.08)	116308 (17.27)	156 (17.25)	9891 (17.26)	14 (16.89)	436 (17.25)

Source: U.P. State Election Officer, Lucknow.

level, there has been an increase of 3.42 per cent of women representatives as Pramukh and 2.5 per cent increase in case of Kshetra Panchayat members. Interestingly, women represented 37.95 per cent, 35.82 per cent and 37.06 per cent respectively as members of Gram Panchayats, Kshetra Panchayats and Zila Panchayats. Similarly, women constituted 35.32%, 36.71% and 53.62% as heads of Gram Panchayats, Kshetra Panchayats and Zila Panchayats in the state.

Table 4.14. Women's Representation in Panchayats (2000) in U.P.

Particular	*Class*	*Women*	*Male*	*Total*
Member Gram Panchayat	ST	0.02	0.03	0.05
	SC	10.34	13.723	24.06
	OBC	10.92	17.79	28.71
	General	16.67	30.52	47.19
	Total	37.95	62.05	100.0
Member Kshetra Panchayat	ST	0.03	0.03	0.00
	SC	8.65	14.93	23.58
	OBC	10.51	19.01	29.52
	General	16.64	30.21	46.85
	Total	35.82	64.18	100.0
Member Zila Panchayat	ST	0.09	0.00	0.09
	SC	9.74	14.72	24.46
	OBC	11.43	19.29	30.72
	General	15.80	28.03	44.73
	Total	37.06	62.94	100.0
Pradhan Gram Panchayat	ST	0.02	0.04	0.06
	SC	8.05	13.71	21.75
	OBC	11.88	21.68	33.56
	General	15.37	29.25	44.62
	Total	35.32	64.68	100.0
Kshetra Panchayat Pramukh	ST	–	–	–
	SC	9.89	10.01	19.90
	OBC	12.73	15.58	28.31
	General	14.09	37.70	51.79
	Total	36.71	63.29	100.0
Adhyaksha Zila Panchayat	ST	–	–	–
	SC	13.04	7.25	20.29
	OBC	15.94	15.94	31.88
	General	24.64	23.19	47.88
	Total	53.62	46.38	100.0

Source: U.P. State Election Commission, Lucknow.

The Panchayat election was held in 2005–06 and women in Panchayati Raj Institutions represented 39.19 per cent. Their share has increased much higher as against the statutory provision of 33 per cent. This has been found more pronouncing in case of Adhyaksha Zila Panchayat (75.71 per cent) followed by Member, Zila Panchayat (51.83 per cent) and Pradhan Village Panchayat (50.22 per cent). A comparative analysis of women representation in Panchayati Raj Institutions shows higher increase in Adhyaksha Zila Panchayat (40.75 percentage points) while at block level, their representation as Block Pramukh increased by 18.54 percentage points. Even there share in the presentation as Village Pradhan has also increased by 17.22 percentage points.

Table 4.15. Women's Representation in Panchayats (2006) in U.P.

S.No.	*Name of Post*	*Reservation Categories of Elected Candidates*				
		ST	*SC*	*OBC*	*General*	*Total*
1.	Member, Village Panchayat	345	69971	85314	94613	250243 (38.40)
2.	Pradhan, Village Panchayat	61	4961	12536	8545	26103 (50.22)
3.	Member, Kshetra Panchayat	53	6340	9219	9268	24880 (38.23)
4.	Member, Zila Panchayat	1	271	409	376	1057 (40.22)
5.	Pramukh, Kshetra Panchayat	1	108	190	125	424 (51.83)
6.	Jyeshtha, Up-Pramukh	0	20	92	136	248 (30.28)
7.	Kanishtha Up-Pramukh	0	37	89	115	241 (24.46)
8.	Adhyaksh, Zila Panchayat	0	10	28	15	53 (75.71)
	TOTAL	461	81718	107877	113193	303249 (39.19)

Table 4.16. Increasing Representation of Women in PRIs

	1995	*2000*	*2005*	*Change*
		Village Panchayat		
Pradhan	33.00	35.32	50.22	17.22
Member	33.32	37.95	38.40	5.08
		Block		
Pramukh	33.29	36.71	51.83	18.54
Member	33.32	35.82	38.23	4.91
		District		
Adhyaksha	34.96	53.62	75.71	40.75
Member	32.36	37.06	40.22	7.16

Source: U.P. State Election Commission, Lucknow.

Problems of Women Representation

In many countries including India, cultural traditions hold many women back from playing prominent role in economic life. Political participation of women, no doubt has increased at the grass root level, however, their participation in parliament and state assemblies continues to remain very low. Their representation is reported to be just 8.5 per cent in parliament, 10.8 per cent in Central Council of Ministers. Their participation in state assemblies has shown a declining trend. In 1984–85, their number was reported to be 141 which declined to 135 in 1987–88 and further to 113 in 1989–90 and 62 in 1993–94. Thus, women's participation in the political institutions and decision making bodies has been reported to be negligible.

In order to ensure gender equity in development planning, women related legislations were enacted to safe-guard the rights and interests of women besides protecting against discrimination, violence, atrocity and also to prevent socially undesirable practices. The legislative support for women in India is shown as follows :

Legislative Support for Women in India

Women Specific Legislations

- The Immoral Traffic (Prevention) Act, 2000
- The Dowry Prohibition Act, 1961
- The Indecent Representation of Women (Prohibition) Act, 1986
- The Commission of Sati (Prevention) Act, 1987
- Women Related Legislations
- The Guardians and Wards Act, 1860
- Indian Penal Code, 1860
- The Christian Marriage Act, 1872
- The Indian Evidence Act, 1872
- The Married Women's Property Act, 1874
- The Workmen's Compensation Act, 1923
- The Legal Practitioners (Women) Act, 1923
- The Indian Succession Act, 1925
- The Child Marriage Restraint Act, 1929
- The Payments of Wages Act, 1936
- The Muslim Personal Law (Shariyat)
- Application Act, 1937
- The Factories Act, 1948
- The Minimum Wages Act, 1948
- The Employee's State Insurance Act, 1948
- The Plantation Labour Act, 1951
- The Cinematograph Act, 1952
- The Special Marriage Act, 1954
- The Hindu Marriage Act, 1955
- The Hindu Adoptions & Maintenance Act, 1956
- The Hindu Minority & Guardianship Act, 1956

- The Hindu Succession Act, 1956
- The Maternity Benefit Act, 1961
- The Beedi and Cigar Workers (Conditions of Employment) Act, 1966
- The Foreign Marriage Act, 1969
- The Indian Divorce Act, 1969
- The Medical Termination of Pregnancy Act, 1971
- Code of Criminal Procedure, 1973
- The Bonded Labour System (Abolition) Act, 1976
- The Equal Remuneration Act, 1976
- The Contract Labour (Regulation and Abolition) Act, 1979
- The Inter–State Migrant Workmen (Regulation of Employment and Conditions of Service) Act, 1979
- The Family Courts Act, 1984
- Juvenile Justice Act, 1986
- The Child Labour (Prohibition and regulation) Act, 1986
- National Commission for Women Act, 1990
- The Infant Milk Substitutes, Feeding Bottles and Infant Foods (Regulation and Production, Supply and Distribution) Act, 1992
- The Pre–Natal Diagnostic Technique (Regulation and Prevention of Misuse) Act, 1994.

Though women have been enthusiastically participating in politics but they have also been facing difficulties, challenges and problems related with their political participation and engagement and initiation of development programmes. Their low level of active participation in implementation of development programmes and schemes and also in political process is the prominent problem for the administrators and policy makers. The proxy in election process, meetings, participation in development programmes and decision making has caused a serious damage to women empowerment and hence concern for all. Husbands, in–laws and close relatives have become the main decision makers relegating the actual women representatives to the background. The role conflict among these representatives has also increased while managing house responsibilities and political activities simultaneously. Since male dominating society is reluctant in accepting the women as decision makers, they are been abused and harassed by officials, caste leaders, elected representatives and also power brokers. They are also facing revengeful attitudinal behaviour in the society since they have defeated influential persons of the other sex. Thus, desire for political power, status and sustainable source of black money has also caused social concern affecting women representatives.

The study is focusing women empowerment through Panchayati Raj Institutions with the help of decentralized governance. The concept of development is being approached by two development models. One is Universalist and the other is Ecological Approach (Model). Max Weber developed Bureaucratic model in Universalist approach where cross cultural relationship is deeply concerned with authority in democracy. Authority plays vital role in the name of bureaucracy. The other ecological model was opined by F.W. Riggs. In developing country like India where fused society is more prevalent than prismatic society because of agrarian society. Ecology of any state always has upper hand in development.

Both states are known as backward states in development process. Thus, it becomes pertinent to analyze their valuable effort in development which can be possible through analytical study of sampled states and districts with their demography, because in this chapter, women representation in Panchayati Raj Institutions have been discussed in empirical form.

5
Election Engineering

(a) Assistance in Election

The research team has made an endeavour to know about the general assistance and help taken by the contestant in the election process. For this assistance purpose, nature of company is classified into five terms, e.g. alone, relative or family members, friends, other local people and former Pradhans or Panchayati Raj Institution members. In Uttar Pradesh, 1.51 per cent and in Chhattisgarh 16.28 per cent members fought elections without taking any support from anyone. They themselves were capable to contest. Maximum representatives 86.36 per cent in Uttar Pradesh and 55.04 per cent in Chhattisgarh were assisted by family members or relatives (Table – 5.1). In some cases, friends also assisted which was 6.06 percent and 7.75 per cent in Uttar Pradesh and Chhattisgarh respectively. Assistance by local people and former PRI members was also seen.

Table 5.1. Assistance in Election

District	Block	Assistance in Election					
		Alone	Family Members/ Relatives	Friends	Other Local People members	Old PRI	Total Pradhan/
Sitapur	Biswan	0.00	88.89	0.00	11.11	0.00	100.0
	Pahla	5.00	95.00	0.00	0.00	0.00	100.0
Gonda	Colonelganj	0.00	60.00	20.00	10.00	10.00	100.0
	Paraspur	0.00	88.89	11.11	0.00	0.00	100.0
	Total	1.51	86.36	6.06	4.56	1.51	100.0
Raipur	Kasdol	27.50	70.00	0.00	2.50	0.00	100.0
	Abhanpur	17.65	58.82	17.65	2.94	2.94	100.0
Bilaspur	Bilha	11.43	48.57	40.00	0.00	0.00	100.0
	Patharia	0.00	30.00	20.00	50.00	0.00	100.0
	Total	16.28	55.04	7.75	20.15	0.78	100.0

(b) Assistance in Visiting Block/ Zila Panchayat :

For the purpose of election process to visit block Headquarters and District Head Quarters, the family members were asked to accompany. Usually they were accompanied by 83.33 per cent and 63.56 percent family members in respective states. Apart from family persons some supporting agencies like friends, 13.65 per cent in Uttar Pradesh and 16.28 per cent in Chhattisgarh participated. This is a significant feature of political interest by family members to promote females in direct democracy system for the upliftment of rural society (Table – 5.2).

Table 5.2. Assistance in Visiting Block/ Zila Panchayats

District	*Block*	*Assistance in Visiting*				
		Alone	*Friends*	*Family Members/ Relatives*	*Old Pradhan/ PRI members*	*Total*
Sitapur	Biswan	0.00	16.67	83.33	0.00	100.0
	Pahla	0.00	15.00	85.00	0.00	100.0
Gonda	Colonelganj	0.00	30.00	60.00	10.00	100.0
	Paraspur	5.56	0.00	94.44	0.00	100.0
	Total	1.51	13.65	83.33	1.51	100.0
Raipur	Kasdol	30.00	0.00	70.00	0.00	100.0
	Abhanpur	20.59	14.71	61.76	2.94	100.0
Bilaspur	Bilha	11.42	34.29	54.29	0.00	100.0
	Patharia	0.00	20.00	70.00	10.00	100.0
	Total	17.83	16.28	63.56	2.33	100.0

(c) Post for Contesting Election

The heads of the district level and intermediate level Panchayats are indirectly elected by the public. In Uttar Pradesh, the representation of the Head of district level is there but it is not so in Chhattisgarh. In case of intermediate level the representation in Uttar Pradesh is nearly 17 per cent while it is nearly 9 per cent in Chhattisgarh. In both the states, the maximum number of respondents are from gram Panchayat level. In Uttar Pradesh, nearly 73 per cent respondents are Pradhan and members of gram Panchayat whereas it is 84 per cent in Chhattisgarh.

Table 5.3. Post for Contesting Election

District	*Block*	*Post*						
		Zila Panchayat		*Kshetra Panchayat*		*Gram Panchayat*		*Total*
		Adhyakshe	*Member*	*Pramukh*	*Member*	*Pradhan*	*Member*	
Sitapur	Biswan	0.00	11.11	0.00	16.67	16.67	55.55	100.0
	Pahla	0.00	5.00	0.00	10.00	20.00	65.00	100.0
Gonda	Colonelganj	10.00	10.00	10.00	20.00	20.00	30.00	100.0
	Paraspur	0.00	11.11	0.00	16.67	16.67	55.55	100.0
	Total	1.51	9.09	1.51	15.15	18.18	54.56	100.0
Raipur	Kasdol	0.00	7.50	2.50	10.00	5.00	75.00	100.0
	Abhanpur	0.00	5.88	0.00	2.94	8.82	82.36	100.0
Bilaspur	Bilha	0.00	8.57	2.86	5.71	5.71	77.15	100.0
	Patharia	0.00	10.00	0.00	10.00	10.00	70.00	100.0
	Total	0.00	7.75	1.55	6.98	6.98	76.74	100.0

(d) Canvassing Support

Family members of the representatives are keen helpers in the canvassing process. 68.18 per cent in Uttar Pradesh have opined that in canvassing they were supported by their family members whereas in Chhattisgarh 45.74 per cent were supported. Friends have also played an important role but after the family members (table – 5.4). 19.70 per cent and 29.46 per cent friends were rather helping in Uttar Pradesh and Chhattisgarh state. Local people were also helpful but their percentage is identical, 9.09 per cent and 9.30 per cent in sampled states.

Table 5.4. Assistance in Canvassing

District	*Block*	*Assistance in Canvassing*						
		Alone	*Friends*	*Family Members/ Relatives*	*Local People*	*Old PRI Members*	*Others*	*Total*
Sitapur	Biswan	0.00	16.67	55.56	22.22	5.55	0.00	100.0
	Pahla	0.00	20.00	80.00	0.00	0.00	0.00	100.0
Gonda	Colonelganj	0.00	40.00	30.00	20.00	10.00	0.00	100.0
	Paraspur	0.00	11.11	88.89	0.00	0.00	0.00	100.0
	Total	0.00	19.70	68.18	9.09	3.03	0.00	100.0
Raipur	Kasdol	25.00	0.00	72.50	2.50	0.00	0.00	100.0
	Abhanpur	11.76	23.53	58.83	2.94	2.94	0.00	100.0
Bilaspur	Bilha	11.43	62.86	14.28	11.43	0.00	0.00	100.0
	Patharia	0.00	40.00	25.00	30.00	5.00	0.00	100.0
	Total	13.95	29.46	45.74	9.30	1.55	0.00	100.0

(e) Local Environment

The research team tried to know about the nature of local atmosphere during the election period. In Chhattisgarh, 90.70 per cent members responded to a peaceful atmosphere while in Uttar Pradesh 68.18 per cent felt peace. Uttar Pradesh looks more sensitive and advanced in political culture because of the proliferation of many political parties (Table – 5.5).

Table 5.5. Local Environment During Election

District	Block	Local Environment				
		Groupism and Group Clashed	Conflicts among different communities	Peaceful Atmosphere	Tense and Violent Atmosphere	Total
Sitapur	Biswan	5.56	0.00	61.11	33.33	100.0
	Pahla	0.00	0.00	75.00	25.00	100.0
Gonda	Colonelganj	20.00	0.00	60.00	20.00	100.0
	Paraspur	27.78	0.00	72.22	0.00	100.0
	Total	12.12	0.00	68.18	19.70	100.0
Raipur	Kasdol	.2.50	0.00	97.50	0.00	100.0
	Abhanpur	11.76	0.00	79.41	8.83	100.0
Bilaspur	Bilha	2.86	0.00	94.28	2.86	100.0
	Patharia	0.00	10.00	90.00	0.00	100.0
	Total	4.65	1.55	90.70	3.10	100.0

(f) Motivation for Election

Motivation is a core component of organizational behaviour. It is a catalyst which expedites and promotes the reaction. Earlier females were supposed to live in closed surroundings but the landmark 73rd Constitutional Amendment has broken the walls and made mandatory provision for the females to come out of for the success of true democracy. Table – 5.6 clearly shows the notion of family members to motivate the elected members. More than 70 per cent (71.21 per cent) of total sample in Uttar Pradesh were motivated by family members while in Chhattisgarh 35.66 per cent were motivated only which is just half in comparison to Uttar Pradesh. Villages in Chhattisgarh were also having the onus of motivation i.e. 26.36 per cent.

Table 5.6. Motivation for Contesting Election

District	Block	Motivation						
		Self	Friends	Family Members/ Relatives	Villagers	Old PRIs Members	More than 1	Total
Sitapur	Biswan	22.22	5.56	66.66	5.56	0.00	0.00	100.0
	Pahla	0.00	10.00	90.00	0.00	0.00	0.00	100.0
Gonda	Colonelganj	10.00	20.00	50.00	0.00	20.00	0.00	100.0
	Paraspur	16.67	5.56	66.66	0.00	0.00	11.11	100.0
	Total	12.13	9.09	71.21	1.51	3.03	3.03	100.0
Raipur	Kasdol	25.00	0.00	70.00	5.00	0.00	0.00	100.0
	Abhanpur	0.00	23.53	32.35	41.18	0.00	2.94	100.0
Bilaspur	Bilha	2.86	31.43	8.57	17.14	0.00	40.00	100.0
	Patharia	0.00	20.00	20.00	60.00	0.00	0.00	100.0
	Total	8.52	17.83	35.66	26.36	0.00	11.63	100.0

(g) Objectives for Contesting Elections

Members were asked about the motive of their contesting election (Table – 5.7). To assess the motive, certain features were classified, namely welfare activity, all-round development, social activities and social justice, improving status of women, etc. In Chhattisgarh, 76.44 per cent members gave their views about all–round development while in Uttar Pradesh, 77.27 per cent have clubbed the issues. Specific or particular issue was not responded to in Uttar Pradesh in majority.

Table 5.7. Objectives Behind Contesting Election

District	*Block*	*Objectives*					
		Promoting welfare activities	*Promoting development*	*Carrying social activities & social justice*	*Improving status of women*	*More than 1*	*Total*
Sitapur	Biswan	22.22	16.67	5.55	0.00	55.56	100.0
	Pahla	5.00	5.0	5.00	0.00	85.00	100.0
Gonda	Colonelganj	10.00	0.00	0.00	0.00	90.00	100.0
	Paraspur	5.56	11.11	0.00	0.00	83.33	100.0
U.P.	Total	10.61	9.09	3.03	0.00	**77.27**	100.0
Raipur	Kasdol	20.00	50.00	5.00	25.00	0.00	100.0
	Abhanpur	0.00	100.0	0.00	0.00	0.00	100.0
Bilaspur	Bilha	0.00	77.14	0.00	2.86	20.00	100.0
	Patharia	0.00	90.00	0.00	0.00	10.00	100.0
Chhatisgarh	Total	6.20	**76.44**	1.55	8.53	6.98	100.0

(h) Frequency of Contesting Elections

In Uttar Pradesh 80.30 per cent and in Chhattisgarh 95.34 per cent elected representatives were contesting for the first time (Table – 5.8). Although, some members had the experience of contesting elections more than one time 16.67 and 3.03 per cent members were contesting elections second and third time in Uttar Pradesh, and 3.10 and 0.78 percent in Chhattisgarh respectively. In both the states, contesting election number of times seems similar, no major changes are found.

Table 5.8. Frequency of Contesting Election

District	Block	Frequency				
		First Time	Second Time	Third Time	Fourth Time	Total
Sitapur	Biswan	88.89	11.11	0.00	0.00	100.0
	Pahla	85.00	5.00	10.00	0.00	100.0
Gonda	Colonelganj	50.00	50.00	0.00	0.00	100.0
	Paraspur	83.33	16.67	0.00	0.00	100.0
U.P.	Total	80.00	16.67	**3.03**	0.00	100.0
Raipur	Kasdol	90.00	5.00	2.50	2.50	100.0
	Abhanpur	97.06	2.94	0.00	0.00	100.0
Bilaspur	Bilha	97.14	2.86	0.00	0.00	100.0
	Patharia	100.0	0.00	0.00	0.00	100.0
Chhatisgarh	Total	95.34	**3.10**	**0.78**	0.78	100.0

(i) Number of Times Elected

Table – 5.9 depicts majority of new entrants in Panchayati Raj Institutions. 90.91 percent members were elected first time in Uttar Pradesh while less than 100 percent (98.45 per cent) were elected in Chhattisgarh. Only 9.09 per cent and 1.55 per cent members were not elected first time in Uttar Pradesh and Chhattisgarh state respectively. This shows significant growth of development through reservation policy in Panchayati Raj Institutions.

Table 5.9. Whether Selected For First Time

District	Block	Selected for first time		
		Yes	No	Total
Sitapur	Biswan	100.00	0.00	100.0
	Pahla	95.00	5.00	100.0
Gonda	Colonelganj	60.00	40.00	100.0
	Paraspur	94.44	5.56	100.0
U.P.	Total	**90.91**	**9.09**	100.0
Raipur	Kasdol	97.50	2.50	100.0
	Abhanpur	97.06	2.94	100.0
Bilaspur	Bilha	100.00	0.00	100.0
	Patharia	100.00	0.00	100.0
Chhatisgarh	Total	**98.45**	**1.55**	100.0

(j) Frequency of Meetings

Members were asked about the frequency of meetings held and attended by them. To analyze the frequency, it has been classified into 6 categories. The majority of people i.e. 60.61 per cent in Uttar Pradesh have participated in the meetings twice (Table – 5.10). But in Chhattisgarh 53.49 per cent have gone to the meetings only once. Few members have never gone to any meeting. Whereas 21.70 per cent Chhattisgarh members have shown their interest in attending the meetings six times which is a landmark of participation.

Table 5.10. Frequency of Meetings

District	*Block*	*Frequency of Meetings*							
		NIL	*One*	*Two*	*Three*	*Four*	*Five*	*Six*	*Total*
Sitapur	Biswan	0.00	33.33	61.11	5.56	0.00	0.00	0.00	100.0
	Pahla	0.00	15.00	80.00	5.00	0.00	0.00	0.00	100.0
Gonda	Colonelganj	10.00	10.00	50.00	30.00	0.00	0.00	0.00	100.0
	Paraspur	0.00	50.00	44.44	0.00	5.56	0.00	0.00	100.0
	Total	1.51	28.79	60.61	7.58	1.51	0.00	0.00	100.0
Raipur	Kasdol	0.00	0.00	2.50	5.00	5.00	17.50	70.00	100.0
	Abhanpur	2.94	79.41	17.65	0.00	0.00	0.00	0.00	100.0
Bilaspur	Bilha	2.86	77.14	20.00	0.00	0.00	0.00	0.00	100.0
	Patharia	0.00	75.00	20.00	5.00	0.00	0.00	0.00	100.0
	Total	1.55	53.49	13.95	2.33	1.55	5.43	21.70	100.0

(k) Accompanying Visit to Block and Zila Panchayat

The nature of company has been categorically defined into three terms namely, alone, family members and others. In Chhattisgarh 17.83 per cent females are bold and courageous to visit alone while in Uttar Pradesh their percentage 1.51 which is negligible. Mostly, women of Uttar Pradesh are accompanied by their respected family members i.e. 92.43 percent. Just more than half 55.81 percent of Chhattisgarh elected women members are accompanied by family members in visiting the head quarter. Apart from the above two categories, others also playing a vital role in accompanying the members to their visits. Chhattisgarh has dominating figure 26.36 per cent females have got the support of others whereas in Uttar Pradesh 6.06 percent are being supported by others (Table – 5.11).

Table 5.11. Accompanied Visit to Block/ Zila Panchayat

District	*Block*	*Accompanied Visits*			
		Alone	*Family Members*	*Others*	*Total*
Sitapur	Biswan	5.56	94.44	0.00	100.0
	Pahla	0.00	100.00	0.00	100.0
Gonda	Colonelganj	0.00	60.00	40.00	100.0
	Paraspur	0.00	100.00	0.00	100.0
	Total	**1.51**	**92.43**	**6.06**	100.0
Raipur	Kasdol	0.00	52.50	47.50	100.0
	Abhanpur	17.65	52.94	29.41	100.0
Bilaspur	Bilha	40.00	48.57	11.43	100.0
	Patharia	15.00	60.00	5.00	100.0
	Total	**17.83**	**55.81**	**26.36**	100.0

1. Distance Covered for Meeting

The research team also questioned regarding the distance covered for meetings. Distance wise it has been divided into groups; within village, upto 5 kms. and more than 5 kms. 71.21 per cent of Uttar Pradesh females enjoy the meetings within the village. Rest 18.18 per cent and 10.61 per cent females use to cover the distance upto 5 kms. and more than 5 kms. respectively. Chhattisgarh females are also not far behind, 65.89 per cent females attend the meeting within the village while 15.50 per cent members cover upto 5 kms. distance for meetings. Approximately one fifth of the total sample, i.e. 18.61 per cent members are used to cover the distance of more than 5 kms. (Table – 5.12).

Table 5.12. Distance Covered for Participating in Meetings

District	*Block*	*Distanc*			
		Within Village	*Upto 5 kms.*	*More than 5 kms.*	*Total*
Sitapur	Biswan	72.22	16.67	11.11	100.0
	Pahla	75.00	25.00	0.00	100.0
Gonda	Colonelganj	50.00	20.00	30.00	100.0
	Paraspur	77.78	11.11	11.11	100.0
	Total	**71.21**	**18.18**	**10.61**	100.0
Raipur	Kasdol	17.50	27.50	55.00	100.0
	Abhanpur	94.12	2.94	2.94	100.0
Bilaspur	Bilha	91.43	5.71	2.86	100.0
	Patharia	70.00	30.00	0.00	100.0
	Total	**65.89**	**15.50**	**18.61**	100.0

Election empowers individuals with their sovereign rights to cast their votes in democracy and thus to sovereign power. Thus, people's powers are to be exercised by the Government for the people themselves. This notion of power is the motive force behind the principle of decentralization.

It is the first step towards decentralized system of power through empowering citizens to form their own government.

6
Impact of Socio-Economic Factors on Decentralization

The appreciation of any study depends upon the presentation of situation analysis of the sample. For the purpose, the research team collected relevant data to depict social, economic, educational and political behavioural aspects of the sample. The focus of the study is on problems of women representatives in Panchayati Raj System of Uttar Pradesh and Chhattisgarh. In Uttar Pradesh: Sitapur and Gonda while in Chhattisgarh: Raipur and Bilaspur districts were selected. Further, two blocks of each district were selected for the in-depth study namely Biswan and Pahla development block of Sitapur, Colonelganj and Paraspur development blocks of Gonda district, Kasdol and Abhanpur development blocks of Raipur district and Bilha and Patharia development blocks of Bilaspur district.

(a) Age Distribution

Age plays a vital role in any study where maturity and behaviour reflects. For the purpose, the total sample is divided into five age groups i.e. less than 25, 25 to 35, 36 to 45, 46 to 55 and more than 55 years. 7.58 per cent respondents are less than 25 years in Uttar Pradesh while 1.55 per cent are in Chhattisgarh. Majority of women representatives belong to 25 to 35 years age group. In Uttar Pradesh 34.85 percent while in Chhattisgarh 30.23 per cent respondents having 25 to 35 years of age. Table 6.1 depicts that one third representatives of the total sample are young, energetic and enthusiastic which is a healthy sign of democracy. In Chhattisgarh, 51.94 per cent women representatives are from 36 to 45 age group which shares more than 50 per cent of the total sample in Chhattisgarh.

Both states represent equal distribution in more than 55 years of age. No representative is found in Biswan development block of Sitapur district in the category of more than 55 years of age.

Table 6.1. Age of the Respondents

District	*Block*	*Age*					
		< 25	*25–35*	*36–45*	*46–55*	*> 55*	*Total*
Sitapur	Biswan	0.00	38.89	27.78	33.33	0.00	100.0
	Pahla	5.00	45.00	30.00	15.00	5.00	100.0
Gonda	Colonelganj	0.00	20.00	20.00	30.00	30.00	100.0
	Paraspur	22.22	27.78	22.22	27.78	0.00	100.0
	Total	**7.58**	**34.85**	**25.75**	**25.75**	**6.07**	100.0
Raipur	Kasdol	5.00	45.00	42.50	2.50	5.00	100.0
	Abhanpur	0.00	20.59	58.82	14.71	5.80	100.0
Bilaspur	Bilha	0.00	31.43	54.29	11.43	2.85	100.0
	Patharia	0.00	15.00	55.00	15.00	15.00	100.0
	Total	**1.55**	**30.23**	**51.94**	**10.08**	**6.20**	100.0

(b) Caste

Seventy third Constitutional Amendment is a landmark development for social engineering. This amendment guarantees caste and gender reservation. In case of gender thirty three per cent seats are reserved for females at each tier in Panchayati Raj. Similarly, caste has also been considered for the upliftment and growth for Decentralized Governance and Panchayati Raj in the country. Schedule Caste women constitute 30.30 per cent in Uttar Pradesh where as in Chhattisgarh there is 24.03 per cent representation. In Scheduled Tribes 10.08 per cent elected women are found while Uttar Pradesh has none as shown in Table – 6.2. Maximum number of women belong to other backward castes. 50.39 per cent of the total sample in Chhattisgarh are from OBC. Approximately just 40 per cent of women of OBC were elected in Uttar Pradesh i.e. 39.39 per cent. By and large women from general category have slightly less representation, 30.31 per cent in Uttar Pradesh. In Chhattisgarh 15.50 per cent women belong to general category.

Table 6.2. Caste of the Respondents

District	*Block*	*Caste*				
		SC	*ST*	*OBC*	*General*	*Total*
Sitapur	Biswan	50.00	0.00	38.89	11.11	100.0
	Pahla	30.00	0.00	65.00	5.00	100.0
Gonda	Colonelganj	20.00	0.00	30.00	50.00	100.0
	Paraspur	16.67	0.00	16.67	66.66	100.0
	Total	**30.30**	**0.00**	**39.39**	**30.31**	100.0
Raipur	Kasdol	10.00	10.00	75.00	5.00	100.0
	Abhanpur	26.47	11.76	55.88	5.89	100.0
Bilaspur	Bilha	31.43	11.43	28.57	28.57	100.0
	Patharia	35.00	5.00	30.00	30.00	100.0
	Total	**24.03**	**10.08**	**50.39**	**15.50**	100.0

(c) Marital Status

Table – 6.3 reveals that majority of elected women are married. In Chhattisgarh, 98.44 per cent women are married whereas in Uttar Pradesh they have a less number i.e. 93.94 per cent. Unmarried women have no interest in political democracy of Panchayati Raj System, by which an inference can be drawn that after marriage women start sharing in the political process and development by the motivation of their in–laws and husband. Widows have poor attitude and response in Panchayati Raj System because 6.06 per cent and 0.78 per cent women were found elected in Uttar Pradesh and Chhattisgarh state respectively.

Table 6.3. Marital Status of the Respondents

District	*Block*	*Marital Status*				
		Married	*Unmarried*	*Widow*	*Separate*	*Total*
Sitapur	Biswan	100.00	0.00	0.00	0.00	100.0
	Pahla	100.00	0.00	0.00	0.00	100.0
Gonda	Colonelganj	80.00	0.00	20.00	0.00	100.0
	Paraspur	88.89	0.00	11.11	0.00	100.0
	Total	**93.94**	0.00	**6.06**	0.00	100.0
Raipur	Kasdol	95.00	2.50	2.50	0.00	100.0
	Abhanpur	100.00	0.00	0.00	0.00	100.0
Bilaspur	Bilha	100.00	0.00	0.00	0.00	100.0
	Patharia	100.00	0.00	0.00	0.00	100.0
	Total	**98.44**	0.78	**0.78**	0.00	100.0

(d) Educational Level

To analyze the educational level, the whole sample has been classified into illiterate, primary, middle, secondary and graduate level (Table – 6.4). Uttar Pradesh depicts a very poor show that 59.09 percent members are illiterate while Chhattisgarh constitutes 21.71 per cent. Primary level educated females are representing 41.86 per cent in Chhattisgarh whereas Uttar Pradesh represents 24.24 per cent of the total sample size. 25.58 per cent of Chhattisgarh women are educated up to middle class which is one fourth of the total sample in the state. In secondary level education, Chhattisgarh females are just the double to Uttar Pradesh i.e. 6.98 per cent and 3.03 per cent respectively. Graduate females have more or less similar percentage which constitutes 3.03 per cent in Uttar Pradesh and 3.87 per cent in Chhattisgarh. There should be some mandatory education level qualification for elected representatives because illiteracy is the main cause for poor governance.

Table 6.4. Educational Level of the Respondents

District	*Block*	*Educational Level*						
		Illite.	*Prim.*	*Midd.*	*Secon.*	*Grad.*	*Other*	*Total*
Sitapur	Biswan	83.33	16.67	0.00	0.00	0.00	0.00	100.0
	Pahla	45.00	35.00	20.00	0.00	0.00	0.00	100.0
Gonda	Colonelganj	50.00	10.00	20.00	20.00	0.00	0.00	100.0
	Paraspur	55.56	27.78	5.55	0.00	11.11	0.00	100.0
	Total	**59.09**	**24.24**	**10.61**	**3.03**	**3.03**	0.00	100.0
Raipur	Kasdol	15.00	47.50	20.00	15.00	2.50	0.00	100.0
	Abhanpur	11.76	55.88	29.41	2.95	0.00	0.00	100.0
Bilaspur	Bilha	22.86	22.86	37.14	5.71	11.43	0.00	100.0
	Patharia	50.00	40.00	10.00	0.00	0.00	0.00	100.0
	Total	**21.71**	**41.86**	**25.58**	**6.98**	**3.87**	0.00	100.0

(e) Occupation

Occupation has been defined in terms of labour, cultivator, pensioner, service, self–employed and housewife. In Uttar Pradesh, 6.06 per cent members are labourerrs while in Chhattisgarh, 3.10 per cent are labourers (Table – 6.5). 22.73 per cent women come in the cultivator category in Uttar Pradesh while Chhattisgarh has 35.66 per cent cultivators. In

Table 6.5. Occupation of the Respondents

District	*Block*	*Occupation*						
		Labour	*Culti-vator*	*Pensi-oner*	*Service*	*Self-employed*	*Other*	*Total*
Sitapur	Biswan	11.11	22.22	0.00	0.00	0.00	66.67	100.0
	Pahla	5.00	25.00	0.00	0.00	0.00	70.00	100.0
Gonda	Colonelganj	10.00	20.00	0.00	0.00	0.00	70.00	100.0
	Paraspur	0.00	22.22	0.00	0.00	0.00	77.78	100.0
	Total	**6.06**	**22.73**	0.00	0.00	0.00	**71.21**	100.0
Raipur	Kasdol	0.00	45.00	0.00	5.00	17.50	32.50	100.0
	Abhanpur	5.88	0.00	0.00	0.00	17.65	76.47	100.0
Bilaspur	Bilha	5.72	65.71	0.00	0.00	8.57	20.00	100.0
	Patharia	0.00	25.00	0.00	0.00	10.00	65.00	100.0
	Total	**3.10**	**35.66**	0.00	**1.55**	13.95	**45.74**	100.0

field study, 1.55 per cent elected members were found in service in Chhattisgarh. 71.21 per cent elected members are housewives in Uttar Pradesh while in Chhattisgarh, housewives constitute only 45.74 per cent.

(f) Nature of Family

Indian society is based on bondings and relationship among family members. Nowadays it has lost its glory especially in urban areas which is commonly known to all of us. In the study, the research team tried to explore the nature of family of the respondents. 56.06 per cent have joint family and 43.94 per cent enjoy nuclear family system in Uttar Pradesh (Table – 5.6). Chhattisgarh also has similar proportion of joint and nuclear family system which is 55.81 per cent and 44.19 per cent respectively.

Table 6.6. Nature of Family of the Respondents

District	Block	Nature of Family		
		Joint	Nuclear	Total
Sitapur	Biswan	44.44	55.56	100.0
	Pahla	60.00	40.00	100.0
Gonda	Colonelganj	70.00	30.00	100.0
	Paraspur	55.56	44.44	100.0
	Total	**56.06**	**43.94**	100.0
Raipur	Kasdol	30.00	70.00	100.0
	Abhanpur	50.00	50.00	100.0
Bilaspur	Bilha	71.42	28.58	100.0
	Patharia	90.00	10.00	100.0
	Total	**55.81**	**44.19**	100.0

(g) Family Size

For the analysis of primary data, members are grouped into five class intervals of family size i.e. 1 to 5, 6 to 10, 11 to 15, 16 to 20 and above 20. Table – 6.7 reveals that 9.09 per cent and 17.05 per cent respondents have the family size upto 5 members in Uttar Pradesh and Chhattisgarh respectively. Between 6 to 10 family members have the maximum number in both the states. 46.97 per cent and 49.61 per cent families have members between 6 to 10 in Uttar Pradesh and Chhattisgarh. More than 10 to 15 family members can be seen in 34.85 per cent and 28.68 per cent in sample states. Family planning concept is not featuring which is the main hurdle in socio-economic development.

Table 6.7. Family Size of the Respondents

District	*Block*	*Total Number of Members in Family*					
		1–5	*6–10*	*11–15*	*16–20*	*> 20*	*Total*
Sitapur	**Biswan**	**11.11**	**50.00**	**27.78**	**11.11**	**0.00**	**100.0**
	Pahla	**5.00**	**40.00**	**40.00**	**5.00**	**10.00**	**100.0**
Gonda	**Colonelganj**	**20.00**	**60.00**	**10.00**	**10.00**	**0.00**	**100.0**
	Paraspur	**5.56**	**44.44**	**50.00**	**0.00**	**0.00**	**100.0**
	Total	**9.09**	**46.97**	**34.85**	**6.06**	**3.03**	**100.0**
Raipur	**Kasdol**	**30.00**	**47.50**	**17.50**	**5.00**	**0.00**	**100.0**
	Abhanpur	**5.889**	**58.82**	**29.42**	**5.88**	**0.00**	**100.0**
Bilaspur	**Bilha**	**17.14**	**40.00**	**40.00**	**2.86**	**0.00**	**100.0**
	Patharia	**10.00**	**55.00**	**30.00**	**5.00**	**0.00**	**100.0**
	Total	**17.05**	**49.61**	**28.68**	**4.66**	**0.00**	**100.0**

(h) Occupation of Family

Generally occupation is a parameter of economic empower-ment in the society by which one can scale the social status too. The principle of need of hierarchy theory is very pertinent in Indian society. In field study occupation has been classified into agriculture, landless labour, pensioners, service, self-employed and others. Maximum numbers are occupied in agriculture according to Table – 6.8. In field study, it was found that 81.82 per cent families of Uttar Pradesh are occupied in agriculture profession. Chhattisgarh state is also not far behind in number i.e. 83.72 per cent. In remaining occupations, 18.61 per cent and 6.20 per cent are landless labourer in state of Uttar Pradesh and Chhattisgarh. 6.06 per cent and 7.75 per cent families have self–employment.

Table 6.8. Main Occupation of Family of Respondents

District	Block	Main Occupation						
		Agri.	Land. Labour	Pensi.	Servi.	Self-Empl.	Other	Total
Sitapur	Biswan	67.67	22.22	0.00	0.00	11.11	0.00	100.00
	Pahla	95.00	0.00	0.00	0.00	0.00	5.00	100.0
Gonda	Colonelganj	90.00	10.00	0.00	0.00	0.00	0.00	100.0
	Paraspur	77.78	11.11	0.00	0.00	11.11	0.00	100.0
	Total	**81.82**	**18.61**	0.00	0.00	6.06	1.51	100.0
Raipur	Kasdol	80.00	2.50	0.00	0.00	17.50	0.00	100.0
	Abhanpur	94.12	2.94	0.00	0.00	2.94	0.00	100.0
Bilaspur	Bilha	77.14	14.29	0.00	5.71	2.86	0.00	100.0
	Patharia	85.00	5.00	5.00	0.00	5.00	0.00	100.0
	Total	**83.7**	**6.20**	0.78	1.55	7.75	0.00	100.0

(i) Average Annual Income

The family of elected members have the maximum income between Rs. 20,000 to 40,000 (Table – 5.9). In this slab, Uttar Pradesh represents 46.96 per cent while Chhattisgarh has less number 31.78 per cent in comparison. Income wise Chhattisgarh is rather poor than Uttar Pradesh. 62.79 per cent

Table 6.9. Average Annual Income of the Respondents

District	Block	Annual Income (in Rs.)						
		Upto 20000	20001–40000	40001–60000	60001–80000	80001–100000	100000 above	Total
Sitapur	Biswan	27.77	61.11	5.56	0.00	5.56	0.00	100.0
	Pahla	5.00	50.00	30.00	10.00	5.00	0.00	100.0
Gonda	Colonelganj	20.00	20.00	40.00	20.00	0.00	0.00	100.0
	Paraspur	0.00	44.44	22.22	27.78	5.56	0.00	100.0
	Total	**12.12**	**46.97**	**22.73**	13.64	4.54	0.00	100.0
Raipur	Kasdol	85.00	10.00	0.00	5.00	0.00	0.00	100.0
	Abhanpur	32.35	58.82	8.83	0.00	0.00	0.00	100.0
Bilaspur	Bilha	65.71	34.29	0.00	0.00	0.00	0.00	100.0
	Patharia	65.00	25.00	10.00	0.00	0.00	0.00	100.0
	Total	**62.79**	**31.78**	**3.88**	1.55	0.00	0.00	100.0

of Chhattisgarh has income upto only Rs. 20,000, whereas in Uttar Pradesh this figure is 12.12 per cent only. More than 40,000 income can also be seen i.e. 22.73 per cent in Uttar Pradesh against 3.88 per cent in Chhattisgarh. Very few families who have attained the slab beyond 60,000 income are there., 13.64 per cent of Uttar Pradesh belong to this slab.Under the social scenario, the functioning of local institutions greatly suffers due to lopsided social equilibrium. The low involvement of women in the development process is the reflection of this problem. There are instances where the local panchayats are in the hands of upper caste men (directly in the capacity of Chairperson, indirectly through dummy candidates), who are not accountable to the community and often utilize local public services for their own benefits.

Due to the number of inequalities (on account of education, profession, ownership etc.) the women suffer in their socio-economic life and that reflects their ability to participate in the village development, while there are a number of issues like fuel, fodder management, drinking water, health and family planning, where women have a vital role to play. So in a way, lack of participation of women has bearing on the abilities of the panchayats to handle these critical issues.

Lack of education is a big hindrance for people to access information and participate in the village development. Also, such disparity deprives many from availing opportunities. The poor among whom the illiteracy is more, are always in a disadvantageous position, and will get less benefit from decentralization unless the programme of improving their capabilities is initiated.

Under the economic perspective, the village rich men, including traders and money lenders have major role in the utilization of village property like forest land, village pond, community land, and so on. For example, the issues like where the school building is to be created, who should be the beneficiary for the rural development schemes, what should be the priority of development, how the village income should be utilized, are influenced by the interests of rich, and may not necessarily be the gram panchayats or gram sabhas. They control the decisions directly or indirectly through the clutches of economic dominance by tilting public opinion in their favour. To be more specific, people depending on the money lenders are hardly going to speak against their wishes, and hesitate to articulate their problems collectively.

7
Problems Faced in Decentralization and Suggestive Measures

PROBLEMS

This chapter emphasizes the main problems of women representatives in working and functioning of political administration. To find out their problems, their responses have been taken into account for analysis.

(a) Participation in Discussions

The research team tried to know about the frequency of participation in discussions. Only 7.58 per cent representatives of Uttar Pradesh regularly participate in discussions while Chhattisgarh represents 75.19 per cent (Table – 7.1). It seems that Chhattisgarh state came into existence recently in

Table 7.1. Participation in Discussion of the Meetings

District	*Block*	*Participation in Discussions*					
		Regularly	*Casually*	*Occasionally*	*Sometimes*	*Never*	*Total*
Sitapur	Biswan	11.11	22.22	11.11	44.45	11.11	100.0
	Pahla	10.00	20.00	35.00	30.00	5.00	100.0
Gonda	Colonelganj	0.00	10.00	30.00	50.00	10.00	100.0
	Paraspur	5.56	5.55	22.22	61.11	5.56	100.0
	Total	**7.58**	**15.15**	24.24	45.45	7.58	100.0
Raipur	Kasdol	80.00	10.00	5.00	5.00	0.00	100.0
	Abhanpur	55.88	8.82	2.94	23.53	8.83	100.0
Bilaspur	Bilha	80.00	20.00	0.00	0.00	0.00	100.0
	Patharia	90.00	0.00	0.00	0.00	10.00	100.0
	Total	**75.19**	**10.86**	2.33	7.75	3.87	100.0

comparison to Uttar Pradesh. So they are more prone and enthusiastic about the nature of work to perform. Females are more casual in participation in both states i.e. 15.15 per cent and 10.86 per cent in Uttar Pradesh and Chhattisgarh respectively. Usually 45.45 per cent representatives of Uttar Pradesh participate in discussion on some lines. This also proves that there is lack of motivation which is very essential to participate for rural growth and upliftment.

(b) Stress During Discussions

More active participation means more stress, but it is not so in case of Chhattisgarh. Table 7.2 shows that 85.27 per cent respondents do not feel any stress during discussion which is a healthy sign for their mental toughness. Females of Uttar Pradesh are also not far behind, 63.63 per cent representatives have shown no stress. Although nature wise, they are more sensitive, soft humans but they try to stick about their verdicts.

Table 7.2. Feeling of Stress During Discussion of the Meetings

District	*Block*	*Feeling of Stress*				
		Regularly	*Some-times*	*Occasio-nally*	*Never*	*Total*
Sitapur	Biswan	0.00	5.55	27.78	67.67	100.0
	Pahla	0.00	5.00	25.00	70.00	100.0
Gonda	Colonelganj	0.00	0.00	60.00	40.00	100.0
	Paraspur	0.00	5.55	27.78	67.67	100.0
	Total	0.00	4.55	31.82	**63.63**	100.0
Raipur	Kasdol	0.00	5.00	5.00	90.00	100.0
	Abhanpur	14.71	11.76	2.94	70.59	100.0
Bilaspur	Bilha	11.43	0.00	0.00	88.57	100.0
	Patharia	5.00	0.00	0.00	95.00	100.0
	Total	7.75	4.65	2.33	**85.27**	100.0

(c) Opportunity for Expressing Views

Respondents are fair enough to provide their opportunity in expressing views. According to Table 7.3 42.64 per cent of Chhattisgarh females are having opportunity most of the time whereas 4.55 per cent have it in Uttar Pradesh. This is co–related with their participation because Chhattisgarh has more representation than Uttar Pradesh. In some time opportunity given Uttar Pradesh females have maximum number i.e., 77.27 per cent. There were 41.08 per cent Chhattisgarh samples which were never given opportunity to express their views. So given and not given opportunity has nearly same proportion in Chhattisgarh.

Table 7.3. Frequency for Giving Opportunity for Expressing Views in Meetings

District	*Block*	*Frequency*			
		Most of the time	*Some-times*	*Never*	*Total*
Sitapur	Biswan	5.55	77.78	16.67	100.0
	Pahla	5.00	80.00	15.00	100.0
Gonda	Colonelganj	0.00	80.00	20.00	100.0
	Paraspur	5.56	72.22	22.22	100.0
	Total	**4.55**	**77.27**	18.18	100.0
Raipur	Kasdol	0.00	7.50	92.50	100.0
	Abhanpur	41.18	26.47	32.35	100.0
Bilaspur	Bilha	85.71	11.43	2.86	100.0
	Patharia	55.00	25.00	20.00	100.0
	Total	**42.64**	16.28	**41.08**	100.0

(d) Cause for Not Giving Opportunity

Education is a key to knowledge. To acknowledge the reason for not giving opportunity has been classified mainly into three groups, namely prohibition by Chairperson, male dominance and lack of knowledge. According to Table – 7.4, Chairperson did not permit to say or express views to 7.54 per cent in Chhattisgarh. Gender bias is also seen in the form of male dominance in both states i.e. 8.33 per cent and 30.19 per cent in Uttar Pradesh and Chhattisgarh states. Main causal factor is lack of knowledge due to poor educational level or illiteracy of elected members. Majority of them 91.67 per cent are not aware about the issues of the discussion so they are supposed to be good listeners instead of active participation in Uttar Pradesh. Though this type of hiatus is also present in Chhattisgarh but their number is 56.60 per cent which is less than that of Uttar Pradesh.

Table 7.4. Reason for Not Giving Opportunity

District	Block	Reasons				
		Not Given Opportunity by chair	Domination of male members	Lack of prior knowledge	Others	Total
Sitapur	Biswan	0.00	33.33	66.67	0.00	100.0
	Pahla	0.00	0.00	100.00	0.00	100.0
Gonda	Colonelganj	0.00	0.00	100.00	0.00	100.0
	Paraspur	0.00	0.00	100.00	0.00	100.0
	Total	0.00	**8.33**	**91.67**	0.00	100.0
Raipur	Kasdol	5.41	16.22	70.27	8.10	100.0
	Abhanpur	9.09	72.73	18.18	0.00	100.0
Bilaspur	Bilha	0.00	0.00	100.00	0.00	100.0
	Patharia	0.00	50.00	50.00	0.00	100.0
	Total	**7.54**	**30.19**	**56.60**	5.67	100.0

(e) Cooperation of Government Officials

In Uttar Pradesh, due to poor participation, selected members have nothing to say about government officials' behaviour. But in Chhattisgarh, 27.91 per cent members have replied that there is excellent cooperation by officials. Most of the samples have given satisfactory remark about the behavior of government officials i.e. 78.79 per cent and 65.11 percent in respective states. In comparison to Chhattisgarh, 21.21 per cent members of Uttar Pradesh have shown resentment about the cooperation of officials.

Table 7.5. Attitude and Cooperation of Government Officials

District	*Block*	*Attitude and Cooperation*				
		Excellent	*Satisfa-ctory*	*Un-Satis-factory*	*Others*	*Total*
Sitapur	Biswan	0.00	72.22	27.78	0.00	100.0
	Pahla	0.00	75.00	25.00	0.00	100.0
Gonda	Colonelganj	0.00	80.00	20.00	0.00	100.0
	Paraspur	0.00	88.89	11.11	0.00	100.0
	Total	0.00	**78.79**	21.21	0.00	100.0
Raipur	Kasdol	90.00	10.00	0.00	0.00	100.0
	Abhanpur	0.00	88.24	11.76	0.00	100.0
Bilaspur	Bilha	0.0	97.14	2.86	0.00	100.0
	Patharia	0.00	80.00	20.00	0.00	100.0
	Total	**27.91**	**65.11**	6.98	0.00	100.0

(f) Consultation on Agenda Matters

Before any formal meeting, an agenda is circulated to the members. But due to ignorance and less awareness, they are bound to consult someone (Table – 7.6). For the consultation, they have more confidence in their family members. 87.88 per cent and 77.52 per cent members have shown high degree of confidence level in their respective family members in Uttar Pradesh and Chhattisgarh. Only 1.51 per cent in Uttar Pradesh approach male members of PRIs for consultation. Similarly in Chhattisgarh where only 4.65 per cent have shown confidence in male PRIs. Thus, in both states members are relying on family persons. Another feature is also seen here that they are not prone to take confidence amongst same sex. Very few members have tried to consult agenda matter with some other female counterparts of PRIs. There were 6.06 per cent of Uttar Pradesh and 2.33 percent of Chhattisgarh females who are trying to take help in consultation with other female Panchayati Raj Institution members.

Table 7.6. Consultation of Agenda Matters

District	Block	Consultation						
		Family Members	PRIs Members (Male)	PRIs Members (Female)	Officials	General Public	Two Options	Total
Sitapur	Biswan	94.44	0.00	5.56	0.00	0.00	0.00	100.0
	Pahla	90.00	0.00	10.00	0.00	0.00	0.00	100.0
Gonda	Colonelganj	80.00	0.00	0.00	0.00	20.00	0.00	100.0
	Paraspur	83.32	5.56	5.56	0.00	5.56	0.00	100.0
	Total	**87.88**	**1.51**	**6.06**	0.00	4.55	0.00	100.0
Raipur	Kasdol	85.00	10.00	0.00	0.00	5.00	0.00	100.0
	Abhanpur	91.18	2.94	0.00	0.00	5.88	0.00	100.0
Bilaspur	Bilha	62.86	2.86	0.00	0.00	0.00	34.28	100.0
	Patharia	65.00	0.00	15.00	0.00	5.00	15.00	100.0
	Total	**77.52**	**4.65**	**2.33**	0.00	3.88	11.62	100.0

(g) Participation in Committees

The working of three tier system in Panchayati Raj is being conducted through committees. Though, the committee system in India is prevalent since colonial rule. Being the elected representatives of PRIs, they are part and parcel for representation and participation in committees. To assess the frequency of participation, it has been classified into regular, sometimes, occasionally and never terms. Uttar Pradesh has very less regular participation i.e. 7.58 per cent whereas in Chhattisgarh 79.85 per cent females participated where it is a regular feature. 24.24 per cent of Uttar Pradesh and 10.85 per cent of Chhattisgarh females replied for sometimes. Maximum number 60.60 per cent occasionally participate in Uttar Pradesh which hampers the pace of growth. Certain members are for the name sake, completely passive and never participate. They constitute 7.58 per cent in Uttar Pradesh and 2.32 per cent in Chhattisgarh of the total sample (Table – 7.7).

Table 7.7. Participation in Committees

District	*Block*	*Participation*				
		Regu-larly	*Some-times*	*Occasio-nally*	*Never*	*Total*
Sitapur	Biswan	11.11	16.67	50.00	22.22	100.0
	Pahla	5.00	10.00	85.00	0.00	100.0
Gonda	Colonelganj	10.00	60.00	30.00	0.00	100.0
	Paraspur	5.55	27.78	61.12	5.55	100.0
	Total	**7.58**	**24.24**	**60.60**	**7.58**	100.0
Raipur	Kasdol	75.07	10.00	15.00	0.00	100.0
	Abhanpur	73.53	14.71	8.82	2.94	100.0
Bilaspur	Bilha	94.29	0.00	0.00	5.71	100.0
	Patharia	75.00	25.00	0.00	0.00	100.0
	Total	**79.58**	**10.85**	**6.98**	**2.32**	100.0

(h) Hindrances in Women Participation

We still believe in feudal system which is inherited through genes. Success of any institution depends upon the human resources, not on infrastructure. Albeit, infrastructure and structure is necessary for conducting the management and administration. Constitution has guaranteed the reservation of females in PRIs for Scheduled Castes, Scheduled Tribes, Other Backward Castes and general category. Here Table – 7.8 depicts the types of hindrances which cause the fair functioning of participation in PRIs. Types were divided into illiteracy, social restrictions, household traditions etc. There were 18.18 per cent and 35.66 per cent respondents in favour of illiteracy in Uttar Pradesh and Chhattisgarh respectively. Social restrictions are also opined by 9.09 per cent in Uttar Pradesh and 11.63 per cent in Chhattisgarh. It means that society does not still permit participation of women in the development process. 3.03 per cent and 10.85 per cent females said that it was due to household work. They do not have spare time for these things. Family custom is also a barrier of women participation in politics, given by 7.58 per cent and 10.08 per cent in Uttar Pradesh and Chhattisgarh. Maximum number 62.12 per cent of Uttar Pradesh have clubbed all hindrances. While in Chhattisgarh, this is just half i.e. 31.78 per cent.

Table 7.8. Hindrances in Women Participation in Politics

District	*Block*	*Hindrances*					
		Illiteracy	*Social Restric-tions*	*Household Works*	*Family Tradi-tions*	*More than 1*	*Total*
Sitapur	Biswan	16.67	5.55	5.55	5.55	66.68	100.0
	Pahla	20.00	10.00	5.00	10.00	55.00	100.0
Gonda	Colonelganj	20.00	10.00	0.00	10.00	60.00	100.0
	Paraspur	16.67	11.11	0.00	5.55	66.67	100.0
	Total	**18.18**	**9.09**	**3.03**	**7.58**	**62.12**	100.0
Raipur	Kasdol	25.00	12.50	22.50	15.00	25.00	100.0
	Abhanpur	41.18	8.82	5.88	8.82	35.30	100.0
Bilaspur	Bilha	34.29	8.57	8.57	8.57	40.00	100.0
	Patharia	50.00	20.00	0.00	5.00	25.00	100.0
	Total	**35.66**	**11.63**	**10.58**	**10.08**	**31.78**	100.0

(i) Problems

Respondents were asked about the problems which they have to face individually. To analyze the problem, different terms were used like community organization, political dominance, lack of training, lack of knowledge and non-cooperative attitude of male members. Around 1.52 per cent and 2.32 per cent female members opined the barrier of community in sample states. According to their verdict community demotivates and harasses them from participation in elections. Political interference also creates this problem. The of local leader plays an important role in selecting the candidate according to the benefit for the concerned political parties. This statement was given by 12.50 per cent in Uttar Pradesh and 3.88 per cent in Chhattisgarh state. "Ignorance is bliss", invincible ignorance is also a great problem for the rural folk. No one takes pain to inculcate them about the election process. In Chhattisgarh, 30.23 percent of the total sample favours this statement. 40.91 percent and 48.48 percent female representatives have annexed about two and three problems respectively in Uttar Pradesh, whereas 37.21 females of Chhattisgarh have clubbed two problems only (Table – 7.9).

Table 7.9. Problems

District	*Block*	*Problems*								
		Community Organization	*Political*	*Dominance*	*Lack of Training*	*Lack of Knowledge*	*Non–Cooperative Attitude of males*	*Two Options*	*Three Options*	*Total*
Sitapur	Biswan	5.56	0.00	0.00	0.00	5.56	0.00	27.77	61.11	100.0
	Pahla	0.00	0.00	0.00	0.00	10.00	0.00	50.00	40.00	100.0
Gonda	Colonelganj	0.00	0.00	0.00	0.00	10.00	0.00	40.00	50.00	100.0
	Paraspur	0.00	0.00	0.00	0.00	11.12	0.00	44.44	44.44	100.0
	Total	1.52	0.00	0.00	0.00	9.09	0.00	40.91	48.48	100.0
Raipur	Kasdol	2.50	12.50	5.00	25.00	37.50	7.50	10.00	0.00	100.0
	Abhanpur	0.00	0.00	0.00	8.83	35.29	5.88	50.00	0.00	100.0
Bilaspur	Bilha	5.71	0.00	0.00	0.00	22.86	0.00	45.71	25.72	100.0
	Patharia	0.00	0.00	0.00	10.00	20.00	0.00	55.00	15.00	100.0
	Total	2.32	3.88	1.55	11.63	30.23	3.88	37.21	9.30	100.0

(j) Nature of Cooperation and Coordination Amongst Participants

Participants have harmony amongst themselves. It was stated that 77.27 per cent of Uttar Pradesh representatives members are cordial among themselves. Though the remaining 22.73 per cent members have different nature and behaviour and are non–supportive. Chhattisgarh has upper hand in cordial relationships because 86.05 per cent members responded for the same. Just only 13.95 per cent members do not believe in cooperation and coordination.

Table 7.10. Nature of Cooperation and Coordination Amongst the Participants

District	*Block*	*Nature*		
		Cordial	*Non–Cordial*	*Total*
Sitapur	Biswan	72.22	27.78	100.0
	Pahla	75.00	25.00	100.0
Gonda	Colonelganj	70.00	30.00	100.0
	Paraspur	88.89	11.11	100.0
	Total	**77.27**	**22.73**	100.0
Raipur	Kasdol	90.00	10.00	100.0
	Abhanpur	82.35	17.65	100.0
Bilaspur	Bilha	85.71	14.29	100.0
	Patharia	85.00	15.00	100.0
	Total	**86.05**	**13.95**	100.0

Major Findings and Suggestions

More than two third of India's population lives in rural areas. For their good governance, Panchayati Raj System is instrumented and is a process of democratic decentralization. Panchayati Raj has a uniform three tier structure at village, block (intermediate) and district level. From the very outset, women involvement in Panchayati Raj Institutions (PRIs) is dominatal by two interrelated themes : representation of women in these bodies and effectiveness and outcome of their participation. The present study is also based upon women participation and the challenges they face. This chapter deals with major findings, suggestions and outcome of the study.

The outcome of various constitutional measures, initiatives undertaken under the various plans and legal measures and social legislation adopted for the upliftment of women's status and achieving overall equality among men and women, has been that the participation of women has been good in availing different levels of educational system, in different categories of occupation in both public as well as private sectors, social, cultural and political activities. Various development programmes and welfare activities and availing of certain amenities of life has been consistently increasing. But in reality terms, the women are still lagging far behind men in availing different facilities and participating in different activities due to widespread forms of social evils and cultural backwardness which are limiting the scope of women to participate in different activities according to their choice, even in the affairs of decision making process on certain matters. Even the rural women are visualized lacking the freedom to participate in various rural development programmes and welfare schemes, which are specially introduced with the intention of improving their socio–economic status, because of lack of freedom from the household, social restriction, prevailing illiteracy and increasing control of male family members over the decision of women.

The 73rd Amendment Act of the Constitution which came into force from April 24, 1993 has proposed that not less than one third of total number of seats to be filled by direct election in Panchayat are to be reserved for women. Moreover, after a decade of reservation policy, it becomes pertinent to analyze the social, economic and political awareness and improvement in status of women at three tier structure of Panchayati Raj Institutions.

The detailed analysis of the various aspects of the study are dealt in earlier portion of the book. Here, we present only major findings which have emerged out of the study.

Major Findings

1. Implementation and execution of reservation policy is carried out at the Block Panchayat level without involving local people.

2. Caste-wise equal distribution is present in Uttar Pradesh. But in Chhattisgarh, the maximum number is in OBC category.
3. In both the states, most elected females are married.
4. Literacy level is very poor in Uttar Pradesh where more than half of the total sample is illiterate. But in Chhattisgarh, nearly 42 per cent elected women are educated upto primary level.
5. More than 50 per cent female elected representative have faith in joint family system.
6. Both the states have a family size between 6 to 10 members.
7. In both the states, the main occupation of the respondents is agriculture.
8. In Uttar Pradesh, maximum females are in the age group of 25 to 35, while in Chhattisgarh, most of the females belong to 36 to 45 age group. It means that Uttar Pradesh has younger females in comparison to Chhattisgarh.
9. Identified reserved seats for women are not provided directly to the local people, instead a list is placed at the notice board at block office.
10. Majority of women are either motivated or forced to contest election of Panchayats by their male counterparts.
11. The participation of women is found to be of a very low level in canvassing for their own candidates.
12. Barring a few places, the local environment was found to be peaceful. Uttar Pradesh being a more politically sensitive state has a tense atmosphere.
13. Family members are more motivated in Uttar Pradesh for elections.
14. Chhattisgarh which is a newly developed state has the main motive of contesting elections as development.

15. Most of the females are elected for the first time in both the states.
16. Family members accompany the elected female representatives to visit block and district head quarters.
17. Participation in meeting is more regular in Chhattisgarh than Uttar Pradesh.
18. Chhattisgarh females have more opportunity to express their views most of the time, whereas in Uttar Pradesh they have sometimes.
19. Government officials have a more cooperative attitude towards female elected members.
20. Chhattisgarh females regularly participate in committees whereas in Uttar Pradesh, females are casual.
21. In a democracy, representatives are expected to nurture the constituencies from where they have been elected. But they are not sure about the availability of the constituencies in future, may refrain from cultivating it in the right earnest.
22. In execution of rural development programmes, e.g. Employment Guarantee Schemes much pressure is mounted by local MLAs and MPs for the selection of the people. They do not have a free hand to execute.
23. Similarly, in preparation of Job Card for below poverty line (BPL), rural people put much pressure on nepotism instead of correct and needy selection.

Suggestions

On the basis of the findings of the present study, we try to offer important suggestions which may be incorporated as the policy measures for achieving desired goals and strengthening women participation popularly.

- Identification and notification of Panchayats and wards as reserved for women candidates should be provided adequately and in time.

- Reservation should be made legally with the involvement of the local people, not from the terms dictated by any political pressure.
- Make them accountable for development programmes at least they should have two terms in continuation.
- Educational level is not a criteria taken into account for the election process. There should be a provision to fix at least some minimum education qualification for the candidates willing to contest the election.
- There should be some meeting term mandatory in terms of numbers where female elected members must be present instead of their male counterparts.
- Frequent training programmes and workshops should be organized at different three tier structure level for awareness purpose.
- Concept and relevance of women reservation should be inculcated through audio–video language model.
- In implementation and execution of development programmes, the physical presence and association of women is a must.
- In training and workshops, the emphasis should be given on compulsory participation for speaking and expressing their views regarding the need of local people.
- They require capacity building programmes.
- Males should be congenial to females in all types of development work, from decision making to implementation. Thus, it needs a clear mind set for helping each other instead of confronting on ego issues.

APPENDICES

APPENDIX I

The Constitution (Seventy Third Amendment) Act, 1992 an Act

Further to amend the Constitution of India

Be it enacted by parliament in the Forty–third year of the Republic of India as follows :

1. (1) This Act may be called the Constitution (Seventy third Amendment) Act, 1992.

(2) It shall come into force on such date as the Central Government may, by notification in the Official Gazette, appoint.

2. After Part VIII of the Constitution, the following Part shall be inserted, namely :

PART IX

THE PANCHAYATS

243 In this Part, unless the context otherwise requires, –

(a) "district" means a district in a State;

(b) "Gram Sabha" means a body consisting of persons registered in the electoral rolls relating to a village comprised within the area of Panchayat at the village level;

(c) "intermediate level" means a level between the village and district levels specified by the Governor of a State by public notification to be the intermediate level for the purpose of this Part;

(d) "Panchayat" means an institution (by whatever name called) of self–government constituted under Article 243B, for the rural areas;

(e) "Panchayat area" means the territorial area of a Panchayat;

(f) "population" means the population as ascertained at the last preceding census of which the relevant figures have been published;

(g) "village" means a village specified by the Governor by public notification to be a village for the purpose of this Part and includes a group of villages so specified.

243A. A Gram Sabha may exercise such powers and perform such functions at the village level as the Legislature of a state may by law, provide.

243B(1) There shall be constituted in every State, Panchayats at the Village, intermediate and district levels in accordance with the provisions of this part.

243(2) Notwithstanding anything in clause (1), Panchayats at the intermediate level may not be constituted in a State having a population not exceeding twenty lakhs.

243C(1) Subject to the provision of this Part, the Legislature of a State may, by law, make provisions with respect to the composition of Panchayats :

Provided that the ratio between the population of the territorial areas of a Panchayat at any level and the number of seats in such Panchayat to be filled by election shall, so far as practicable, be the same throughout the State.

243C(2) All the seats in a Panchayat shall be filled by persons chosen by direct election from territorial constituencies in the Panchayat area and; for this purpose, each Panchayat area shall be divided into territorial constituencies in such manner that the ratio between the population of each constituency and the number of seats allotted to it shall, so far as possible, be the same throughout the Panchayat area.

243C(3) The Legislature of a State may, by law, provide for the representation

(a) of the Chairpersons of the Panchayats at the village level, in the Panchayats at the intermediate level or, in the case of a State not having Panchayats at the intermediate level, in the Panchayats at the district level;

(b) of the Chairpersons of the Panchayats at the intermediate level, in the Panchayats at the district level;

(c) of the members of the House of the People and the members of the Legislative Assembly of the State representing constituencies which comprise wholly or partly a Panchayat area at a level other than the village level, in such Panchayat;

(d) of the members of the Council of States and the members of the Legislative Council of the State, where they are registered as electors within –

(i) a Panchayat area at the intermediate level, in Panchayat at the intermediate level;

(ii) a Panchayat area at the district level, in Panchayat at the district level;

243C(4) The Chairperson of a Panchayat and other members of a Panchayat whether or not chosen by direct election from territorial constituencies in the Panchayat area shall have the right to vote in the meeting of the Panchayat.

243C(5) The Chairperson of –

(a) a Panchayat at the village level shall be elected in such manner as the Legislature of a State may, by law, provide; and

(b) a Panchayat at the intermediate level or district shall be elected by, and from amongst the elected members thereof.

243D(1) Seats shall be reserved for

(a) The Scheduled Castes; and

(b) The Scheduled Tribes

in every Panchayat and the number of seats so reserved shall bear, as nearly as may be, the same proportion to the total number of seats to be filled by direct election in that Panchayat as the population of the Scheduled Castes in that Panchayat area or the Scheduled Tribes in that Panchayat area bears to the total population of that area and such seats may be allotted by rotation to different constituencies in Panchayat.

243D(2) Not less than one-third of the total number of seats reserved under clause (1) shall be reserved for women belonging to the Scheduled Castes, or as the case may be, the Scheduled Tribes.

243D(3) Not less than one–third (including the number of seats reserved for women belonging to the Scheduled Castes and the Scheduled Tribes) of the total number of seats to be filled by direct election in every Panchayat shall be reserved for women and such seats may be allotted by rotation to different constituencies in a Panchayat.

243D(4) The offices of the Chairperson in the Panchayat at the village or any other level shall be reserved for the Scheduled Castes, the Scheduled Tribes and Women in such manner as the Legislature of a State may, by law, provide :

Provided that the number of offices of Chairpersons reserved for the Scheduled Castes and the Scheduled Tribes in the Panchayats at each level in any state shall bear, as nearly as may be, the same proportion to the total number of such offices in the Panchayats at each level as the population of the Scheduled Castes in the State or of the Scheduled Tribes in the State bears to the total population of the State:

Provided further that not less than one-third of the total number of offices of Chairpersons in the Panchayat at each level shall be reserved for women :

Provided also that the number of offices reserved under this clause shall be allotted by rotation to different Panchayats at each level.

243D(5) The reservation of seats under clause (1) and (2) and the reservation of offices of Chairpersons (other than the reservation for women) under clause (4) shall cease to have effect on the expiration of the period specified in Article 334.

243D(6) Nothing in this part shall prevent the Legislature of a State from making any provision for reservation of seats in any Panchayat or offices of Chairpersons in the Panchayats at any level in favour of backward class of citizens.

243E(1) Every Panchayat, unless sooner dissolved under any law for the time being in force, shall continue for five years from the date appointed for its first meeting and no longer.

243E(2) No amendment, of any law for the time being in force shall have the effect of causing dissolution of a Panchayat at any level, which is functioning immediately before such amendment, till the expiration of its duration specified in clause (1).

243E(3) An election to constitute a Panchayat shall be completed :

(a) Before the expiry of its duration specified in clause (1);

(b) Before the expiration of a period of six months from the date of its dissolution;

Provided that where the remainder of the period for which the dissolved Panchayat would have continued is less than six months, it shall not be necessary to hold any election under this clause for constituting the Panchayat for such period.

243E(4) A Panchayat constituted upon the dissolution of a Panchayat before the expiration of its duration shall continue only for the remainder of the period for which the dissolved Panchayat would have continued under clause (1) had it not been so dissolved.

243F(1) A person shall be disqualified for being chosen as, and for being, a member of a Panchayat –

(a) If he is so disqualified by or under any law for the time being in force for the purposes of elections to the Legislature of the State concerned;

Provided that no person shall be disqualified on the grounds that he is less than twenty–five years of age, if he has attained the age of twenty–one years.

(b) If he is so disqualified by or under any law made by the Legislature of the State.

243F(2) If any question arises as to whether a member of a Panchayat has become subject to any of the disqualifications mentioned in clause (1), the question shall be referred for the decision of such authority and in such manner as the Legislature of a State may, by law, provide.

243G. Subject to the provisions of this Constitution, the Legislature of a State may, by law, endow the Panchayats with such powers and authority as may be necessary to enable them to function as institutions of self–government and such law may contain provisions for the devolution of powers and responsibilities upon Panchayats at the appropriate level, subject to such conditions as may be specified therein, with respect to–

(a) the preparation of plans for economic development and social justice;

(b) the implementation of schemes for economic development and social justice as may be entrusted to them including those in relation to the matters listed in the Eleventh Schedule.

243H. The Legislature of a State may, by law, –

(a) authorize a Panchayat to levy, collect and appropriate such taxes, duties, tolls and fees in accordance with such procedure and subject to such limits;

(b) assign to a Panchayat such taxes, duties, tolls and fees levied and collected by the State Government for such purposes and subject to such conditions and limits;

(c) provide for making such grants–in–aid to the Panchayats from the Consolidated Fund of the State; and

(d) provide for constitution of such Funds for crediting all money received, respectively, by or on behalf of the Panchayats and also for the withdrawal of such moneys therefrom as may be specified in the law.

243–I(1) The Governor of a State shall, as soon as may be within one year from the commencement of the Constitution (Seventy–Third Amendment) Act, 1992, and thereafter at the expiration of every fifth year, constitute a Finance Commission to review the financial position of the Panchayats and to make recommendations to the Governor as to –

(a) the principles which should govern –

(i) the distribution between the State and Panchayats of the net proceeds of the taxes, duties, tolls and fees leviable by the State, which may be divided between them under this Part and the allocation between the Panchayats at all levels of their respective shares of such proceeds;

(ii) the determination of the taxes, duties, tolls and fees which may be assigned to, or appropriated by, the Panchayats;

(iii) the grants–in–aid to the Panchayats from the Consolidated Fund of the State;

(b) the measures needed to improve the financial position of the Panchayats;

(c) any other matter referred to the Finance Commission by the Governor in the interests of sound finance of the Panchayats.

243–I(2) The legislature of a State may, by law, provide for the composition of the Commission, the qualifications which shall be requisite for appointment as members thereof and the manner in which they shall be selected.

243–I(3) The Commission shall determine their procedure and shall have such powers in the performance of their functions as the Legislature of the State may, by law, confer on them.

243–I(4) The Governor shall cause every recommendation made by the Commission under this Article together with an explanatory memorandum as to the action taken thereon to be laid before the Legislature of the State.

243J. The Legislature of the State may, by law, make provisions with respect to the maintenance of accounts by the Panchayats and the auditing of such accounts.

243K(1) The superintendence, direction and control of the preparation of electoral rolls for, and the conduct of, all elections to the Panchayats shall be vested in a State Election Commission consisting of a State Election Commissioner to be appointed by the Governor.

243K(2) Subject to the provisions of any law made by the Legislature of a State, the conditions of service and tenure of office of the State Election Commissioner shall be such as the Governor may by rule determine :

Provided that the State Election Commissioner shall not be removed from his office except in like manner and on the like grounds as a Judge of a High Court and the conditions of service of the State Election Commissioner shall not be varied to his disadvantage after his appointment.

243K(3) The Governor of a State shall, when so requested by the State Election Commission make available to the State Election Commission such staff as may be necessary for the discharge of the functions conferred on the State Election Commission by clause (1).

243K(4) Subject to the provisions of this Constitution, the Legislature of a State may, by law, make provision with respect to all matters relating to, or in connection with, elections to the Panchayats.

243L. The provisions of this Part shall apply to the Union Territories and shall in their application to a Union Territory, have effect as if the references to the Governor of a State were references to the administrator of the Union Territory appointed under Article 239 and references to the Legislature of the Legislative Assembly of a State were references, in relation to a Union Territory having a Legislative Assembly, to that Legislative Assembly :

Provided that the President may, by public notification, direct that the provisions of this Part shall apply to any Union Territory or part thereof subject to such exceptions and modifications as he may specify in the notification.

243M (1) Nothing in this Part shall apply to the Scheduled Areas referred to in clause (1), and the tribal areas referred to in clause (2) of Article 244.

243M(2) Nothing in this Part shall apply to –

(a) the States of Nagaland, Meghalaya and Mizoram

(b) the hill areas in the State of Manipur for which District Councils exist under any law for the time being in force.

243M (3) Nothing in this Part –

(a) relating to Panchayats at the district level shall apply to the hill areas of the District of Darjeeling in the State of West Bengal for which Darjeeling Gorkha Hill Council exists under any law for the time being in force;

(b) shall be constructed to affected the functions and powers of Darjeeling Gorkha Hill Council constituted under such law.

243M(4) Notwithstanding anything in this constitution–

(a) the Legislature of a State referred to in sub–clause (a) of clause (2) may, by law, extend this Part to that State, except the areas, if any referred to in clause(1) if the Legislative Assembly of that State passes a resolution to that effect by a majority of the total membership of that House and by a majority of not less than two-thirds of the members of that House present and voting.

(b) Parliament may, by law, extend the provisions of this Part to the Scheduled Areas and the tribal areas referred to in clause (1) subject to such exceptions and modifications as may be specified in such law, and so much law shall be deemed to be an amendment of this Constitution for the purpose of Article 368.

243N. Notwithstanding anything in this Part, any provision of any law relating to Panchayats in force in a State immediately before the commencement of the Constitution (Seventy Third Amendment)Act, 1992 which is inconsistent with the provisions of this Part, shall continue to be in force until amended or repealed by a competent Legislature or other competent authority or until the expiration of one year from such commencement, whichever is earlier :

Provided that all the Panchayats existing immediately before such commencement shall continue till the expiration of their duration, unless sooner dissolved by a resolution passed to that effect by the Legislative Assembly of that State or, in the case of a State having a Legislative Council, by each House of the Legislature of that State.

243–O. Notwithstanding anything in this Constitution, –

(a) the validity of any law relating to the delimitation of constituencies or the allotment of seats to such constituencies made or purporting to be made under Article 243K, shall not be called in question in any court;

(b) no election to any Panchayat shall be called in question except by an election petition presented to such authority and in such manner as is provided for by or under any law made by the Legislature of a State.

3. In clause (3) of Article 280 of the Constitution, after sub–clause (b), the following sub–clause shall be inserted, namely :

"(bb) the measures needed to augment the Consolidated Fund of a State to supplement the resources of the Panchayats in the State on the basis of the recommendations made by the Finance Commission of the State;"

4. After the Tenth Schedule to the Constitution, the following Schedule shall be added, namely : –

"Eleventh Schedule
(Article 243G)

1. Agriculture, including agricultural extension.
2. Land improvement, implementation of land reforms, land consolidation and soil conservation.
3. Minor irrigation, water management and watershed development.
4. Animal husbandry, dairying and poultry.
5. Fisheries.
6. Social forestry and farm forestry.
7. Minor forest produce.
8. Small scale industries, including food processing industries.
9. Khadi, village and cotton industries.
10. Rural housing.
11. Drinking water.
12. Fuel and fodder.
13. Roads, culverts, bridges, ferries, waterways and other means of communication.
14. Rural electrification, including distribution of electricity.
15. Non–conventional energy resources.
16. Poverty alleviation programme.

17. Education, including primary and secondary schools.
18. Technical training and vocational education.
19. Adult and non–formal education.
20. Libraries.
21. Cultural activities.
22. Markets and fairs.
23. Health and sanitation, including hospitals, primary health centres and dispensaries.
24. Family welfare.
25. Women and child development.
26. Social welfare, including welfare of the handicapped and mentally retarded.
27. Welfare of the weaker sections, and in particular of the Scheduled Castes and the Scheduled Tribes.
28. Public distribution system.
29. Maintenance of community assets".

APPENDIX II
The Constitution (Seventy-Fourth Amendment) Act, 1992
An Act

Further to amend the Constitution of India.

BE it enacted by Parliament in the Forty–third Year of the Republic of

India as follows :

1. **Short title and commencement** – (1) This Act may be called the Constitution (Seventy–fourth Amendment) Act, 1992.

(2) It shall come into force on such date as the Central Government may, by notification in the Official Gazette, appoint.

2. **Insertion of new Part IXA** – After Part IX of the Constitution, the following Part shall be inserted, namely :

PART IXA

THE MUNICIPALITIES

243P. Definitions – In this Part, unless the context otherwise requires –

(a) "Committee" means a Committee constituted under article 243S;

(b) "district" means a district in a State;

(c) "Metropolitan area" means an area having a population of ten lakhs or more, comprised in one or more districts and consisting of two or more Municipalities or Panchayats or other contiguous areas, specified by the Governor by public notification to be a Metropolitan area for the purposes of this Part;

(d) "Municipal area" means the territorial area of a Municipality as is notified by the Governor;

(e) "Municipality" means an institution of self–government constituted under article 243Q;

(f) "Panchayat" means a Panchayat constituted under article 243B;

(g) "population" means the population as ascertained at the last preceding census of which the relevant figures have been published.

243Q. Constitution of Municipalities. – (1) There shall be constituted in every State, –

(a) A Nagar Panchayat (by whatever name called) for a transitional area, that is to say, an area in transition from a rural area to an urban area;

(b) A Municipal Council for a smaller urban area; and

(c) A Municipal Corporation for a larger urban area, in accordance with the provisions of this Part:

Provided that a Municipality under this clause may not be constituted in such urban area or part thereof as the Governor may, having regard to the size of the area and the municipal services being provided or proposed to be provided by an industrial establishment in that area and such other factors as he may deem fit, by public notification, specify to be an industrial township.

(2) In this article, "a transitional area", "a smaller urban area" or "a larger urban area" means such area as the Governor may, having regard to the population of the area, the density of the population therein, the revenue generated for local administration, the percentage of employment in non–agricultural activities, the economic importance or such other factors as he may deem fit, specify by public notification for the purposes of this Part.

243R. Composition of Municipalities – (1) Save as provided in clause (2), all the seats in a Municipality shall be filled by persons chosen by direct election from the territorial constituencies in the Municipal area and for this purpose each Municipal area shall be divided into territorial constituencies to be known as wards.

(2). The Legislature of a State may, by law, provide–

(a) for the representation in a Municipality of–

(i) persons having special knowledge or experience in Municipal administration;

(ii) the members of the House of the People and the members of the Legislative Assembly of the State representing constituencies which comprise wholly or partly the Municipal area;

(iii) the members of the Council of States and the members of the Legislative Council of the State registered as electors within the Municipal area;

(iv) the Chairpersons of the Committees constituted under clause (5) of Article 243S:

Provided that the persons referred to in paragraph (i) shall not have the right to vote in the meetings of the Municipality;

(b) the manner of election of the Chairperson of a Municipality.

243S. Constitution and composition of Wards Committees, etc. – (1) There shall be constituted Wards Committees, consisting of one or more wards, within the territorial area of a Municipality having a population of three lakhs or more.

(2) The Legislature of a State may, by law, make provision with respect to–

(a) the composition and the territorial area of a Wards Committee;

(b) the manner in which the seats in a Wards Committee shall be filled.

(3) A member of a Municipality representing a ward within the territorial area of the Wards Committee shall be a member of that Committee.

(4) Where a Wards Committee consists of–

(a) one ward, the member representing that ward in the Municipality; or

(b) two or more wards, one of the members representing such wards in the Municipality elected by the members of the Wards Committee,

shall be the Chairperson of that Committee.

(5) Nothing in this Article shall be deemed to prevent the Legislature of a State from making any provision for the constitution of Committees in addition to the Wards Committees.

243T. Reservation of seats. – (1) Seats shall be reserved for the Scheduled Castes and the Scheduled Tribes in every Municipality and the number of seats so reserved shall bear, as nearly as may be, the same proportion to the total number of seats to be filled by direct election in that Municipality as the population of the Scheduled Castes in the Municipal area or of the Scheduled Tribes in the Municipal area bears to the total population of that area and such seats may be allotted by rotation to different constituencies in a Municipality.

(2) Not less than one–third of the total number of seats reserved under clause (1) shall be reserved for women belonging to the Scheduled Castes or, as the case may be, the Scheduled Tribes.

(3) Not less than one–third (including the number of seats reserved for women belonging to the Scheduled Castes and the Scheduled Tribes) of the total number of seats to be filled by direct election in every Municipality shall be reserved for women and such seats may be allotted by rotation to different constituencies in a Municipality.

(4) The officers of Chairpersons in the Municipalities shall be reserved for the Scheduled Castes, the Scheduled Tribes and women in such manner as the Legislature of a State may, by law, provide.

(5) The reservation of seats under clauses (1) and (2) and the reservation of offices of Chairpersons (other than the reservation for women) under clause (4) shall cease to have effect on the expiration of the period specified in article 334.

(6) Nothing in this Part shall prevent the Legislature of a State from making any provision for reservation of seats in any Municipality or offices of Chairpersons in the Municipalities in favour of backward class of citizens.

243U. Duration of Municipalities, etc. – (1) Every Municipality, unless sooner dissolved under any law for the time being in force, shall continue for five years from the date appointed for its first meeting and no longer:

Provided that a Municipality shall be given a reasonable opportunity of being heard before its dissolution.

(2) No amendment of any law for the time being in force shall have the effect of causing dissolution of a Municipality at any level, which is functioning immediately before such amendment, till the expiration of its duration specified in clause (1).

(3) An election to constitute a Municipality shall be completed,–

(a) before the expiry of its duration specified in clause (1);

(b) before the expiration of a period of six months from the date of its dissolution:

Provided that where the remainder of the period for which the dissolved Municipality would have continued is less than six months, it shall not be necessary to hold any election under this clause for constituting the Municipality for such period.

(4) A Municipality constituted upon the dissolution of a Municipality before the expiration of its duration shall continue only for the remainder of the period for which the dissolved Municipality would have continued under clause (1) had it not been so dissolved.

243V. Disqualifications for membership. – (1) A person shall be disqualified for being chosen as, and for being, a member of a Municipality–

(a) if he is so disqualified by or under any law for the time being in force for the purposes of elections to the Legislature of the State concerned:

Provided that no person shall be disqualified on the ground that he is less than twenty five years of age, if he has attained the age of twenty–one years;

(b) if he is so disqualified by or under any law made by the Legislature of the State.

(2) If any question arises as to whether a member of a Municipality has become subject to any of the disqualifications mentioned in clause (1), the question shall be referred for the decision of such authority and in such manner as the Legislature of a State may, by law, provide.

243W. Powers, authority and responsibilities of Municipalities, etc. – Subject to the provisions of this Constitution, the Legislature of a State may, by law, endow–

(a) the Municipalities with such powers and authority as may be necessary to enable them to function as institutions of self–government and such law may contain provisions for the devolution of powers and responsibilities upon Municipalities, subject to such conditions as may be specified therein, with respect to–

(i) the preparation of plans for economic development and social justice;

(ii) the performance of functions and the implementation of schemes as may be entrusted to them including those in relation to the matters listed in the Twelfth Schedule;

(b) the Committees with such powers and authority as may be necessary to enable them to carry out the responsibilities conferred upon them including those in relation to the matters listed in the Twelfth Schedule.

243X. Power to impose taxes by, and Funds of, the Municipalities. – The Legislature of a State may, by law,–

(a) authorise a Municipality to levy, collect and appropriate such taxes, duties, tolls and fees in accordance with such procedure and subject to such limits;

(b) assign to a Municipality such taxes, duties, tolls and fees levied and collected by the State Government for such purposes and subject to such conditions and limits;

(c) provide for making such grants–in–aid to the Municipalities from the Consolidated Fund of the State; and

(d) provide for constitution of such Funds for crediting all moneys received, respectively, by or on behalf of the Municipalities and also for the withdrawal of such moneys therefrom.

as may be specified in the law.

243Y. Finance Commission. – (1) The Finance Commission constituted under Article 243–I shall also review the financial position of the Municipalities and make recommendations to the Governor as to–

(a) the principles which should govern–

(i) the distribution between the State and the Municipalities of the net proceeds of the taxes, duties, tolls and fees leviable by the State, which may be divided between them under this Part and the allocation between the Municipalities at all levels irrespective of the shares of such proceeds;

(ii) the determination of the taxes, duties, tolls and fees which may be assigned to, or appropriated by, the Municipalities;

(iii) the grants–in–aid to the Municipalities from the Consolidated Fund of the State;

(b) the measures needed to improve the financial position of the Municipalities;

(c) any other matter referred to the Finance Commission by the Governor in the interests of sound finance of the Municipalities.

(2) The Governor shall cause every recommendation made by the Commission under this article together with an explanatory memorandum as to the action taken thereon to be laid before the Legislature of the State.

243Z. Audit of accounts of Municipalities. – The Legislature of a State may, by law, make provisions with respect to the maintenance of accounts by the Municipalities and the auditing of such accounts.

243ZA. Elections to the Municipalities. – (1) The superintendence, direction and control of the preparation of electoral rolls for, and the conduct of, all elections to the Municipalities shall be vested in the State Election Commission referred to in Article 243K.

(2) Subject to the provisions of this Constitution, the Legislature of a State may, by law, make provision with respect to all matters relating to, or in connection with, elections to the Municipalities.

243ZB. Application to Union territories. – The provisions of this Part shall apply to the Union territories and shall, in their application to a Union territory, have effect as if the references to the Governor of a State were references to the Administrator of the Union territory appointed under Article 239 and references to the Legislature or the Legislative Assembly of a State were references in relation to a Union territory having a Legislative Assembly, to that Legislative Assembly:

Provided that the President may, by public notification, direct that the provisions of this Part shall apply to any

Union territory or part thereof subject to such exceptions and modifications as he may specify in the notification.

243ZC. Part not to apply to certain areas. – (1) Nothing in this Part shall apply to the Scheduled Areas referred to in clause (1), and the tribal areas referred to in clause (2), of article 244.

(2) Nothing in this Part shall be construed to affect the functions and powers of the Darjeeling Gorkha Hill Council constituted under any law for the time being in force for the hill areas of the district of Darjeeling in the State of West Bengal.

(3) Notwithstanding anything in this Constitution, Parliament may, by law, extend the provisions of this Part to the Scheduled Areas and the tribal areas referred to in clause (1) subject to such exceptions and modifications as may be specified in such law, and no such law shall be deemed to be an amendment of this Constitution for the purposes of Article 368.

243ZD. Committee for district planning. – (1) There shall be constituted in every State at the district level a District Planning Committee to consolidate the plans prepared by the Panchayats and the Municipalitiies in the district and to prepare a draft development plan for the district as a whole.

(2) The Legislature of a State may, by law, make provision with respect to–

(a) the composition of the District Planning Committees;

(b) the manner in which the seats in such Committees shall be filled:

Provided that not less than four–fifths of the total number of members of such Committee shall be elected by, and from amongst, the elected mambers of the Panchayat at the district level and of the Municipalities in the district in proportion to the ratio between the population of the rural areas and of the urban areas in the district;

(c) the functions relating to district planning which may be assigned to such Committees;

(d) the manner in which the Chairpersons of such Committees shall be chosen.

(3) Every District Planning Committee shall, in preparing the draft development plan,–

(a) have regard to–

(i) matters of common interest between the Panchayats and the Municipalities including spatial planning, sharing of water and other physical and natural resources, the integrated development of infrastructure and environmental conservation;

(ii) the extent and type of available resources whether financial or otherwise;

(b) consult such institutions and organisations as the Governor may, by order, specify.

(4) The Chairperson of every District Planning Committee shall forward the development plan, as recommended by such Committee, to the Government of the State.

243ZE. Committee for Metropolitan planning. – (I) There shall be constituted in every Metropolitan area a Metropolitan Planning Committee to prepare a draft development plan for the Metropolitan area as a whole.

(2) The Legislature of a State may, by law, make provision with respect to–

(a) the composition of the Metropolitan Planning Committees;

(b) the manner in which the seats in such Committees shall be filled:

Provided that not less than two–thirds of the members of such Committee shall be elected by, and from amongst, the elected members of the Municipalities and Chairpersons of the Panchayats in the Metropolitan area in proportion to the ratio between the population of the Municipalities and of the Panchayats in that area;

(c) the representation in such Committees of the Government of India and the Government of the State and of such organisations and institutions as may be deemed necessary for carrying out the functions assigned to such Committees;

(d) the functions relating to planning and coordination for the Metropolitan area which may be assigned to such Committees;

(e) the manner in which the Chairpersons of such Committees shall be chosen.

(3) Every Metropolitan Planning Committee shall, in preparing the draft development plan,–

(a) have regard to–

(i) the plans prepared by the Municipalities and the Panchayats in the Metropolitan area;

(ii) matters of common interest between the Municipalities and the Panchayats, including co–ordinated spatial planning of the area, sharing of water and other physical and natural resources, the integrated development of infrastructure and environmental conservation;

(iii) the overall objectives and priorities set by the Government of India and the Government of the State;

(iv) the extent and nature of investments likely to be made in the Metropolitan area by agencies of the Government of India and of the Government of the State and other available resources whether financial or otherwise;

(b) consult such institutions and organisations as the Governor may, by order, specify.

(4) The Chairperson of every Metropolitan Planning Committee shall forward the development plan, as recommended by such Committee, to the Government of the State.

243ZF. Continuance of existing laws and Municipalities.– Notwithstanding anything in this Part, any provision of any law relating to Municipalities in force in a State immediately before the commencement of THE CONSTITUTION (Seventy–fourth Amendment) Act, 1992, which is inconsistent with the provisions of this Part, shall continue to be in force until amended or repealed by a competent Legislature or other competent authority or until the expiration of one year from such commencement, whichever is earlier:

Provided that all the Municipalities existing immediately before such commencement shall continue till the expiration of their duration, unless sooner dissolved by a resolution passed to that effect by the Legislative Assembly of that State or, in the case of a State having a Legislative Council, by each House of the Legislature of that State.

243ZG. Bar to interference by courts in electoral matters.– Notwithstanding anything in this Constitution,–

(a) the validity of any law relating to the delimitation of constituencies or the allotment of seats to such constituencies, made or purporting to be made under article 243ZA shall not be called in question in any court;

(b) no election to any Municipality shall be called in question except by an election petition presented to such authority and in such manner as is provided for by or under any law made by the Legislature of a State.'

3. Amendment of Article 280.– In clause (3) of Article 280 of the Constitution, sub–clause (c) shall be relettered as sub–clause (d) and before sub–clause (d) as so relettered, the following sub–clause shall be inserted, namely:–

"(c) the measures needed to augment the Consolidated Fund of a State to supplement the resources of the Municipalities in the State on the basis of the recommendations made by the Finance Commission of the State;".

4. Addition of Twelfth Schedule.–After the Eleventh Schedule to the Constitution, the following Schedule shall be added, namely:–

"TWELFTH SCHEDULE
(Article 243W)

1. Urban planning including town planning.
2. Regulation of land–use and construction of buildings.
3. Planning for economic and social development.
4. Roads and bridges.
5. Water supply for domestic, industrial and commercial purposes.
6. Public health, sanitation conservancy and solid waste management.
7. Fire services.
8. Urban forestry, protection of the environment and promotion of ecological aspects.
9. Safeguarding the interests of weaker sections of society, including the handicapped and mentally retarded.
10. Slum improvement and upgradation.
11. Urban poverty alleviation.
12. Provision of urban amenities and facilities such as parks, gardens, playgrounds.
13. Promotion of cultural, educational and aesthetic aspects.
14. Burials and burial grounds; cremations, cremation grounds and electric crematoriums.

15. Cattle pounds; prevention of cruelty to animals.
16. Vital statistics including registration of births and deaths.
17. Public amenities including street lighting, parking lots, bus stops and public conveniences.
18. Regulation of slaughter houses and tanneries."

EXTRACT OF ARTICLE 243 I & 243 K FROM CLAUSE 2 OF THE CONSTITUTION (73rd AMENDMENT) ACT, 1992 WHICH ARE REFERRED TO IN THE CONSTITUTION (74TH AMENDMENT) ACT, 1992

243–I. Constitution of Finance Commission to review financial position.

(1) The Governor of a State shall, as soon as may be within one year from the commencement of the Constitution (Seventy–third Amendment) Act, 1992 and thereafter at the expiration of every fifth year, constitute a Finance Commission to review the financial position of the Panchayats and to make recommendations to the Governor as to–

(a) the principles which should govern –

  (i) the distribution between the State and the Panchayats of the net proceeds of the taxes, duties, tolls and fees leviable by the State, which may be divided between them under this part and the allocation between the Panchayats at all levels of their respective shares of such proceeds;

  (ii) the determination of the taxes, duties, tolls and fees which may be assigned to, or appropriated by, the Panchayats;

  (iii) the grants–in–aid to the Panchayats from the Consolidated Fund of the State;

(b) the measures needed to improve the financial position of the Panchayats;

(c) any other matter referred to the Finance Commission by the Governor in the interests of sound finance of the Panchayats.

(2) The Legislature of a State may, by law, provide for the composition of the Commission, the qualifications which shall be requisite for appointment as members thereof and the manner in which they shall be selected.

(3) The Commission shall determine their procedure and shall have such powers in the performance of their functions as the Legislature of the State may by law, confer on them.

(4) The Governor shall cause every recommendation made by the Commission under this Article together with an explanatory memorandum as to the action taken thereon to be laid before the Legislature of the State.

243K. Elections to the Panchayats. (1) The Superintendence, direction and control of the preparation of electoral rolls for, and the conduct of, all elections to the Panchayats shall be vested in a State Election Commission consisting of a State Election Commissioner to be appointed by the Governor.

(2) Subject to the provisions of any law made by the Legislature of a State, the conditions of service and tenure of office of the State Election Commissioner shall be such as the Governor may by rule determine;

Provided that the State Election Commissioner shall not be removed from his office except in like manner and on the like grounds as Judge of a High Court and the conditions of service of the State Election Commissioner shall not be varied to his advantage after his appointment.

(3) The Governor of a State shall, when so requested by the State Election Commission, make available to the State Election Commission such staff as may be necessary for the discharge of the functions conferred on the State Election Commission by Clause (1).

(4) Subject to the provisions of this Constitution, the Legislature of a State may, by law, make provision with respect to all matters relating to, or in connection with elections to the Panchayats.

Bibliography

Approach Paper to Ninth Five Year Plan, 1997, Planning Commission, Govt. of India, New Delhi.

Approach Paper to the Ninth Five Year Plan, 1997.

Bhargava, B.S., *Panchayati Raj Institutions, An Analysis of Issues.*

Dandvate, Madhu, 1997, *Ethos of Planning and Plan Implementation in India.*

First Five Year Plan, 1952, Government of India, New Delhi, p. 223.

Ghosh, Arun, 1985.

Gupta, D.N., *Decentralization Need for Reforms*, 2004.

Jain, L.C. et.al., 1985, *Grass without Roots – Rural Development Under Government Auspices*, New Delhi, Sage, p. 28.

James D. Thompson, Organizations and Output Transactions, in Elihu Katz and Brenda Danet (eds.) *Bureaucracy and the Public*, Basic Books Inc. Publishers, New York, 1973.

James L. Gibson, Hohn M. Iyawevich and James H. Donnelly, Jr., *Organizations : Structure, Processes, Behaviour*, Business Publications, Dallas, Texas, 19734, p. 138.

James W. Fesler, Approaches to the Understanding of Decentralization, *Journal of Politics*, XXVII, August 1965.

James, D. Thompson, *Organizations in Action*, McGraw–Hill Book Company, New York, 1967, p. 76.

Kabra, K.N., 1997.

Kamat, A.R., 1974, D.R. Gadgil, The Last Phase, *Economic & Political Weekly*, Vol. IX, No. 26, p. 1029.

Kaufran Roger A., *Educational System Planning*, Prentice Hall Inc., New Jersey, 1972.

Kurian, C.J., 1978.

Kabra, K.N., 1997, p. 14.

Manfred Kochen and Karl W. Deutsch, Toward a Rational Theory of Decentralization : Some Implications of a Mathematical Approach, *American Political Science Review*, 63, 1969, pp. 734–49.

Mathai, John, Village Government in British India, p. 1.

Mehtra, Balraj, 1988 (May), *The Tribune.*

Minhas, B.S., 1974, op.cit, p. 3.

Oomen, T.K., 2002, Rationalizing fiscal federalism vis–a–vis Rural Local Governments, *Panchayati Raj Update.*

Paul R. Lawrence and Jay W. Lorsch, Differentiation and Integration in Complex Organizations, *Administrative Science Quarterly*, Vol. 12, June 1967.

Report of the Commission on Centre–State Relations, 1988, Government of India, New Delhi.

Report of the Department of Rural Development, 1978–79, Government of India, New Delhi.

Report of the Working Group on Block Level Planning, 1978, Government of India, New Delhi.

Report of the Working Group on District Planning, 1984, p. 21.

Report of the Working Group on District Planning, 1985, Vol. 122, Planning Commission, Government of India, New Delhi.

Second Five Year Plan, 1956, Government of India, New Delhi, pp. 235–245.

Second Five Year Plan, 1956, p. 164.

Second Five Year Plan, 1956, Summary, Government of India, New Delhi, Chap. VII, p. 53.

See, in this connection, the Special Issue of *Public Administration Review*, Vol. XXXII, October, 1972.

Sixth Five–Year Plan, 1980, Government of India, New Delhi.

Vaish (Dr.), B.P., *Panchayati Raj in U.P.*, p. 2.

Index

N

O

P